MW01232369

No Lesser
Glory

Walking with God
in the Hard Places

BY
DR. TIM MAYNARD

Reneé

Grateful for your friendly!

Blessings
Pastor Tim

No Lesser
Glory

Walking with God
in the Hard Places

BY
DR. TIM MAYNARD

ISBN: 978-0-9962685-9-2

DESIGNED & PUBLISHED BY:
Right Eye Graphics
311 Henry Clay Blvd.
Ashland, Kentucky 41101
(606) 393-4197
righteyegraphics.com

Dedicated to my incredible,
loving family, who walked with
me through the hard places.

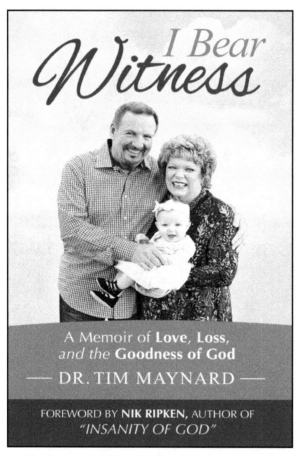

Dr. Tim Maynard authored *I Bear Witness: A Memoir of Love, Loss, and the Goodness of God* in 2018. The book can be purchased online at ibearwitnessbook.com or at Fruit Cove Baptist Church.

Fruit Cove Baptist Church
501 SR 13
Jacksonville, FL 32259

TABLE OF CONTENTS

For I am persuaded that the troubles of this present time will not be worthy to be compared to the glory about to be revealed.

— Romans 8:18

PREFACE

We as a modern day Christian community do not like to think much about suffering, even though it eventually visits every home…every body of worshipers…many every week. Much of what we tend to sing about under the glare of laser lights and smoke machines in contemporary praise and worship in churches leans more toward the positive, upbeat side of our walk with Jesus. But the most telling thing the Bible uses to describe the One we are singing about was "He was a man of sorrows, and acquainted with grief." (Isaiah 53). If Jesus had hired a PR firm, they would no doubt have advised him to downplay that part of His public image.

Sometimes we suppress that part of the person and ministry of Jesus, though He Himself told his followers that He was going to a cross to die and be raised again the third day.

We don't fill auditoriums on Sunday morning with songs or messages about how to suffer like Jesus. Bookstores are replete with most other subjects, but few are catalogued under "Suffering Well." "How to Hurt Like Jesus." You get my gist.

Our theology of suffering is lacking, according to leading missiologist Dr Nik Ripken. It is partly so because we don't really want to think about it as a normal part of the Christian walk. It is also because it doesn't market or sell well in popular Christian culture today.

We step around suffering as though it was an abnormal part of what it means to be a believer, when the Bible (both Old and New Testaments) centralize it in nearly every event and character's life. It's not that we don't read or study about suffering because we know how to handle it. Just the opposite. We don't because we just do not want to dwell too deeply on it.

Perhaps we may think that something is terribly wrong with the universe if we are not enjoying every day, and every experience to its fullest. Suffering exempts us from that.

You won't go far in your Christian experience before you encounter the ugly reality that the experience of suffering is not avoidable. Understanding it's value, appropriating it's fruit, drawing nourishment from it's lessons is optional. Experiencing it is not.

So with a candid admission, this book may skew a little toward "the dark side" for some tastes. If that is your judgement, I would suggest you come back and read it when the truckload of pain and heartache lands in your home or life, or that of someone you love. You may find it helpful then.

I, like most, would prefer to avoid pain at all costs. I would like to keep bees in my backyard, but really don't believe the raw honey to be worth the price of bee stings. Most things of value come at a price. We will not become the ennobled, ruling people of God..a kingdom of priests and kings who will one day judge angels....that He intends for His adopted children's eternity without a few "stings" along the way... including the "sting" of death.

This book was begun in the Fall of 2017 out of the crucible of walking with my wife Pam, who as I wrote some parts of the book you are now holding was suffering the excruciating and withering struggle with a Stage 4 glioblastoma... terminal brain cancer. Many times through the preparation of this manuscript I have had to stop for a while as memories flooded back. And to be candid, I write this as on-going therapy for myself as I grieve, and out of a desire to more completely understand our story and tell it. (For a more thorough telling of the story, see my first book *I Bear Witness*)

But as I finish the final chapters and manuscript of this book, over eighteen months has transpired from the time of my wife's death. As I complete these chapters and the manuscript, I am writing just a few miles south of the devastation brought by Hurricane Michael in the fall of 2018. Tens of thousands of people have lost lives, family, homes and livelihood. For many, life will never return to the "normal" they knew before.

Much of this book also arises out of the experience of shepherding hurting people for almost 40 years as a pastor. It is bathed in tears mingled with the truth that suffering leaves us trying to recover a "normal" we can no longer know.

Finally, this book is not a book of Twitter- ready statements and easy answers. It will ask questions that have no easy answers. It will be transparent and human...at times painfully so as I wrestle with these questions myself. I end with a favorite Scripture verse that we will return to several times in the book: "For I am persuaded that the troubles of this present time will not be worthy to be compared to the glory about to be revealed."

And it is to that present and yet-to-be revealed glory that I hope to bear witness to in this book...and it is no lesser glory!

—Tim Maynard
Sandestin, Florida
2018

INTRODUCTION

Skydiving can be an exhilarating experience. The feeling of actual flight as your body falls through the air; the wind in your face. Exhilarating. So I am told. I have never jumped out of a perfectly functioning airplane in my life, and really do not plan to ever do so. But people do it all the time, and actually enjoy it. Well, most do.

Joan Murray is a forty-seven-year-old bank executive who had successfully completed thirty-five jumps. An article in "Skydiving.com" explains that she was going for her thirty-sixth jump when the unexpected happened. It was early fall of 1999. A perfect sky beckoned her and a multi-colored blanket of fall leaves covered the landscape below. Approximately 14,500 feet below. A perfect day except for what was about to happen.

As her jump and free fall from the plane commenced, her speed increased beyond what she had expected. She was falling through the air so quickly that her primary chute didn't open when she pulled the ripcord. Experienced skydivers prepare for this eventuality and always pack a reserve chute on their jumps. Unfortunately for Joan, her reserve chute also wouldn't release.

Trying frantically to untangle the chute while plummeting through the air at eighty miles per hour, she finally succeeded at about seven hundred feet above the ground. It was enough to break her fall slightly, but only slightly.

The fall crushed her body, primarily her right side where she made impact. The force of her landing was so great it knocked every filling in her mouth loose. As she lay dying on the ground, another reality hit her: She had landed on a massive colony of active fire ants which began stinging her body over and over, and she was helpless to move away from them.

The rescue team found her badly injured but still alive. She was taken by ambulance to the Carolinas Medical Center in Charlotte, North Carolina. Joan remained there in a coma for two weeks, her one hundred-fifteen pound body swollen with fluids as she lingered between life and death.

But another thing perplexed her medical team. Where did all the stings and bites come from that covered her body? Over two hundred of them! They finally determined the marks were from fire ants, and it was then that they realized an amazing thing: The fire ants probably saved her life. The electric shock from the stings of these insects had provided enough stimulus to keep her heart beating until the rescue squad arrived.

Six weeks later, she was released from the hospital and recovered from the majority of her injuries sustained in the fall. And in July 2001 she successfully completed her thirty-seventh jump!

No one could ever have imagined that these horrific little insects with their tormenting bites would have been responsible for her survival. Maybe singer Kelly Clarkson had it right when she sang, "What Doesn't Kill You Makes You Stronger!"

My friend Nik Ripken sent me a photo of a plaque he found on old barn wood which changed that familiar saying just a little. The plaque said, "I don't know if this is killing me or making me stronger!" It hit me at a time in my life when I was asking that very question! My daughter Allison had a friend make a copy of the plaque for me. It arrived the morning my wife passed away. Sometimes it makes you wonder: Am I getting stronger when I feel so defeated and weak? Is this killing me or making me stronger?

Another common saying is one we often use to describe a difficult circumstance: "Stuck between a rock and a hard place." This is not a hopeful statement in itself. It actually conveys a sense of impending doom, of helplessness, of being trapped with no way out. It is how climber Aron Ralston felt when he found himself trapped by a boulder during a climbing accident. His "way out" was to amputate his trapped and necrotic left hand with a pocket knife and no anesthesia, graphically described in his autobiography *Between a Rock and a Hard Place*.

It also describes the circumstance of the Israelites trapped between the Red Sea with the onslaught of Pharaoh's army of terminators coming to finish them off. The only way out was through trust in God and walking straight into the Red Sea. So they trusted and God made a way. The Lord came through for them and the sea parted, drowning Pharaoh's army as the waters receded.

Paul knew about living in the hard places. But he also knew the One Who was Lord even in the midst of the hard places! His resume is colored by experiences in the abyss of despair, peril, disease, persecution, spiritual attack, false accusation, injustice, imprisonment, and physical limitation. He could be the patron saint of every person who suffers, because he had pretty much been through it all!

He spoke of this candidly in the inspired writing of his second letter to the Corinthian church. In 2 Corinthians 4:13, he speaks of being "hard pressed on every side." In other words, he said he was "between a rock and a hard place" as that phrase can legitimately be translated. He gives us clear insight on how to process our times in the hard place. His counsel has been, if you would, "road tested."

As I read his testimony, I find it bracketed by the words, "therefore we do not lose heart." What's the key to surviving the "hard places" of life? Don't lose heart. Don't give up. Don't give in. Don't quit. Cling tenaciously to your faith. God is clinging tenaciously to you, and has promised that "As your days so shall your strength be..." and "underneath are the everlasting arms." (Deuteronomy 33:25, 27). Walk with God in the hard places.

INTRODUCTION

We have an unshakeable bedrock beneath us as we stand upon the Rock....as we build our lives on that foundation, and not the "sinking sand" of our own strength. An elderly African American preacher would remind his small congregation each week of a massive truth. HE would say, "Brothers and sisters, I often trembles upon the rock, but the rock never trembles under me."

You may be in that place today, that hard place, where you find yourself "trembling upon the rock." But I know you will find, as we did, that the ROCK will never, ever tremble under you.

PART ONE:

WALKING WITH GOD IN THE HARD PLACE

In Time of Trouble Say:

First, He brought me here; it is by His will I am in this strait place: in that fact I will rest.

Next, He will keep me here in His love, and give me grace to behave as His child.

Then, He will make the trial a blessing, teaching me the lessons He intends me to learn, and working in me the grace He means to bestow.

Last, In His good time He can bring me out again – how and when He knows.

Let me say I am here,
(1) By God's appointment.   (2) In his keeping.
(3) Under His training.   (4) For His time.

—Andrew Murray

CHAPTER ONE:

A VIEW FROM THE PIT

The guide who met me at the gate of Port-at-Prince International airport led me to his van, filled with dignitaries from the Confederation of Baptists in Haiti. The men, all dressed in suits despite the withering Caribbean heat, sat packed in the seats of the older model van with a broken air conditioner, waiting for me. I was serving in a denominational leadership role, and was there on a visit for a few days to see their work and visit a few orphanages.

On the winding road up to the house where I would stay, we passed the rubble of a concrete structure that had collapsed during the earthquake in Haiti in 2010. It still lay in shambles years later. But as we slowly passed by, the driver spoke quietly and said, "I was under that building for four days."

The van grew quiet. Idle chatter in English and Creole stopped. He told the story that several already knew of his life and death encounter in that quake. His was one of the success stories. He survived and was rescued from the rubble of his mud and concrete grave.

In broken English accentuated with Creole he continued. "I laid beneath the darkness of concrete. I could not move, and there was no light. God was gracious and a trickle of water would occasionally drip in to the confined and dark place. I would wait until enough water came down to make my throat and mouth wet and I would cry out for help as much as I could. I didn't know if it was daytime or night. I didn't know if the sounds I heard were there for me, or if no one knew I was there. I slept. I drank dirty water. I cried out to God. I waited. And on the fourth day, some people moved a rock to allow me to have air and light. They kept digging. And God rescued me."

Four days....crying out....no light....water occasionally dripping in. We sat silently as he unfolded his ordeal. We tried to imagine for a moment what kind of experience that must have been buried within that darkened tomb....then closed the window on our imagination to that dark place. We agreed in thanksgiving to God that he was indeed rescued by Jesus. His world had collapsed....and so perhaps has the world that you are living in today.

Our Experience in the Pit

Our experience in the pit...under the rubble of a life collapse... began in November of 2016 with a numb finger. My wife, Pam, had complained, following a bout with a nasty cold, that she couldn't feel the tip of her index finger. This numbness soon began to affect, not only her finger, but several others fingers as well. Ultimately the limited use of her hand caused by the numbness required her to take a leave from her position as a nurse and as a church instrumentalist and pursue a surgical solution. Carpal tunnel surgery, we thought, would do it. But after the surgery her hand and fingers remained numb. And one day a walk with our granddaughter revealed a problem with her right leg. Now, we knew there was something more going on and set up an appointment with a neurologist and scheduled an MRI.

An experienced neurosurgeon at Mayo Clinic reviewed the scan of her neck and back and said, "the problem is higher up." We both knew that "higher up" meant the brain. We were terrified by the implications but a few days later she lay down again for a second MRI scan... this time of her brain. As she emerged from the test the radiology tech told us, "you are to go immediately to the neuro office." We walked in silence down the hallway to the sliding glass doors where his office was located and were escorted back without sitting down. The pictures were already up on his computer screen and I knew immediately that this was not going to be an easy "no problem don't worry" kind of visit. It wasn't. He showed us the white circle on the scan images. "I'm looking at a brain tumor," he said. "It's three centimeters, and it looks like an advanced stage glioma." We sat stunned. "Because of it's location I wouldn't touch it," he added. "But then, I'm not a tumor surgeon. Get another opinion." We learned later he was right. It was a Stage 4 glioblastoma....basically an incurable and sometimes inoperable tumor.

For us in that moment as well as in the days to follow, life moved into a different dimension. Everything was coming together for us. We had enjoyed our granddaughter McCail for almost a year. Pam's career was moving toward retirement after forty years in surgical nursing. We were celebrating our 40th wedding anniversary in a month. And then, the truck hit us.

I've been hit by a truck before. Stuck in traffic on the interstate while returning from the airport, I sat pinned in at the bottom of an exit ramp on I95 southbound outside of Jacksonville, Florida. A semi, fully loaded, came off the ramp, and seeing the traffic stopped tried to slow his rig without shifting the load. It shifted. He couldn't fully stop and slammed the back of my 2001 Honda Accord.

I never saw him coming. I remember the impact from behind, and in a strange slow-motion experience, saw everything not fastened down in my car...my briefcase, coffee cup, pens, and other assorted items...floating in mid-air as I was thrown toward the windshield. Whether an angel of God or an old trucker's instincts saved me, the rear of my car collapsed but I was able to emerge unscathed. And, amazingly, I drove away! Dazed a bit, but otherwise unharmed by the experience. I had been hit by a truck! A semi! And survived.

This "truck" was not much different. Hearing a doctor use the words "brain" and "tumor" and "late stage" in the same conversation moved our life from normal and a little concerned to slow motion and emotionally paralyzed. We left the appointment stunned with the words "inoperable tumor" etched across our future. The shattered pieces of our life were floating around us.

We were stoic when we left the appointment and somehow found our car. The emotion flooded out on our ride home. We needed windshield wipers for our eyes as the tears streamed down our faces. We talked, we discussed how to tell the family, how to tell the church we had led for almost 25 years that this is happening. We couldn't find words at the moment.

There is a promise that when we cannot find words, the Spirit intercedes for us with words that cannot be uttered (Romans 8:26). I reminded God often of His promise about that through this time. It was good to know because my words were not flowing. This was too deep for the English language to express. But we knew that our God had not...and would not...fail us in this critical moment.

In the days to follow, we learned about crying out from the bottom of the pit.

When You Find Yourself in the Pit

Pits do not have a positive connotation in most languages...unless it's a place where bar-b-que is smoked. My first encounter with a "pit" was in my neighborhood in an empty lot when I was a child. A utility company or construction firm had come and dug, with bright yellow heavy machinery, a deep hole. I'm still to this day not sure what it was for, but I remember well standing on the side of that ominous hole in the ground that seemed to go down for eternity. An abyss. A darkness. A mystery. A pit.

My older companions would sometimes threaten to throw us in "the pit" to scare us, and they told us it was the gateway to the bad place... you know; "h-e-double toothpicks." We surmised that it may go to the center of the earth, or maybe to China! I did not want to go the double-toothpicks place or to China. Nobody wanted to be caught alone without their getaway bike equipped with extra baseball cards and clothes pins with them when exploring near the pit, to add extra horsepower if needed! Mostly we avoided it, even though the mystery on occasion beckoned us to come and peer over the edge and into the darkness.

But as we learn growing older, pits in life are unavoidable. Sometimes, like ours, life goes from sunshine in one moment to the dark, slippery pit of hardship in the next. Other times, the decline to the pit is gradual....the "slippery slope" of a situation that lands you on the bottom in the "miry clay."

In February of 2017, we were in worship. This was the first Sunday following my wife's realization that, due to the disability in her right hand, playing in the orchestra was impossible. It was a hard Sunday for us both... .but especially for Pam. She knew this meant she was not going to be a part of the upcoming Easter musical this year. She sat with a friend and I could see her, midway back in the sanctuary, weeping during the music as she watched her substitute sitting at her instrument and playing her part.

Though I found out later that her tears were genuinely tears of worship more than of regret, I stood before the congregation after the last song had finished. Just before I stood up, something in the words of the chorus we were singing resonated in me and brought to mind Psalm 40:1-3, which says...

I waited patiently for the Lord
he inclined to me and heard my cry.

He drew me up from the pit of destruction,
out of the miry bog,
and set my feet upon a rock,
making my steps secure.

He put a new song in my mouth,
a song of praise to our God.
Many will see and fear,
and put their trust in the Lord.

This Psalm became the framework of my pastoral prayer that morning, and I prayed thinking about my wife and her inability to be on the platform performing in worship. I wept as I looked at her, knowing her heart was breaking, and spoke the words of the inspired Psalmist, little knowing that this Psalm was going to become the outline of what would be the final stage of our journey together in life. I thought I was being pastoral. In reality, I was being prophetic but didn't know it at the time.

Crying Out from the Pit

We don't really know the full historic context of Psalm 40. We do know it speaks of desperation, hopeful prayer, and Divine deliverance, followed by a promise of a testimony from the delivered and a "new song" being sung. According to some Biblical commentators, it is a life map for all of God's children at some point along the journey. It is not the only Psalm that resounds with that theme. Roughly forty-eight passages in the Old Testament deal with them.

But it spoke volumes to our souls through this journey. It did so first by describing the depths of the pit. This was no ordinary "hole" the Psalmist was occupying. This was a place of darkness, despair, helplessness and distress.

In the Old Testament, Joseph found himself thrown into a pit by his jealous brothers. This pit was a cistern used to store water. It was not a solid concrete holding tank. It was cut out of rock and then covered with a lid to prevent an enemy from poisoning the contents or a stray animal from falling in and drowning, thus polluting the precious water. We aren't told in Genesis, but the pit where Joseph was imprisoned by his brothers likely also held water at one time.

Jeremiah the prophet was also imprisoned in a pit. When he would not speak a favorable word to agree with a ruler, his influence was deemed dangerous to the people. He was lowered into a muddy hole where water was held. A pit. A place where he feared he might die...

.sinking to the bottom of the hole with a mouth full of mud.

Whatever geologists or archaeologists tell us about the pit, we do know this. It was a place from which there was no escape....not without help. The walls were often slimy or slick sandstone. The floor was "miry clay." No crawling out in your own strength. There was no solid place to find a foothold. There was no way out without rescue.

It left you with one solution, and one means of escape: Call out for deliverance...for Divine rescue....for help. And then wait patiently for the Lord until He answers.

Promises in the Pit

I thought about my Haitian friend's story as I've read this Psalm over and over in every possible translation through our journey. Four days! Four days without food, clean air, or water and without the promise that anyone was left alive on the surface to look for him. But patiently, trusting and anticipating rescue, he waited. And he waited. And water dripped slowly again as he cried out for help....for God....for deliverance.

I thought about one of the pastors of my home church who told the story of a miraculous comeback to ministry following fifteen years of agonizing and debilitating heart problems. He told of lying in bed many times in the dark of night of his soul in pain... begging God to take his life. Fifteen years.

How long does deliverance take? Sometimes four days....sometimes fifteen years. Sometimes, for reasons only God can explain, it doesn't come in the way we had hoped it would...if we see it at all in our lifetime. The Psalm begins with a hard statement: "I waited patiently for the Lord...." If waiting patiently is a precondition for deliverance, then we were in trouble because patience was not a strength for either of us. But we were about to learn an important lesson.

CHAPTER TWO:

WAITING IN THE HARD PLACE

Waiting is a necessary but difficult part of life. Whether stuck in traffic, or waiting on an elevator, or waiting for a medical diagnosis or for a mate to come along, or waiting for word of an adoption....waiting is part of living. Waiting well is an option. Waiting patiently is hard.

If you've ever been stuck in an elevator whose doors won't open, or that stopped between floors for no known reason, you know what I'm talking about. Thankfully they have phones you can use to call for help, but you still have to wait. And it's hard, even knowing rescue is on the way.

Pam and I had always been activists. Not political ones, but doers. We did things. We got things done. We were both impatient people. And we didn't wait well. Our lives were busy, our work load got done, and then we looked for more. Stopping never came easy. Often it never came at all.

Until the diagnosis hit us. Suddenly, everything we did skidded to a halt. Everything we were involved in was put on pause. Our plans for Pam's retirement, our trip for our fortieth wedding anniversary, our plans to spend time spoiling our granddaughter and caring for our aging parents; It all just stopped. We just stopped. Life as we had known it just stopped.

After we had returned home from rehab, my brother Mark made an insightful observation during a visit with us. As we talked about being "sidelined" by this event....we can't work, can't serve the church in worship, Pam is no longer a nurse and I am a pastor on pause...he said, "It's almost like everything that gave you identity has been taken from you." And he was right. It had. All we had was each other....and Jesus. Our identity now was where it should have been all along: in Christ alone.

Tim Keller told of meeting with a man in New York where he pastored who had lost his car, his house, his job, and was on the verge of losing his wife. He said, "Tim, you don't know that Jesus is all you need until Jesus is all you've got, and then you learn that He is enough." We were at that place. Jesus was all we had to cling to. And so we clung.

And we waited. We waited because waiting is all you can do when you're in the pit. Been there? How do you do with waiting?

We Should Wait Patiently

Most of us wait anxiously. We wait impatiently. We honk our horns at people who don't squeal their tires and pull away when they're in front of us at the red light because, after all, we are important and have places to be. We want to throw our expensive cell phones in the water when they don't respond as quickly as we'd like. We get impatient standing in front of a microwave oven that takes longer than two minutes to heat our meal. We don't need training to anxiously wait.

But waiting patiently is another thing altogether. Waiting patiently involves confidence in the one for whom we are waiting. God's track record alone should instill patience in those of us who are His children. God never fails. God always shows up. God never leaves us, in fact. He is good. We may struggle sometimes with believing that. I purchased a book one time just because I liked the title, which was the longest book title I had ever seen: *"God Has Never Failed Me, But He's Sure Scared Me to Death a Few Times."*

Some wait angrily. When things don't go our way, we lash out at God or at others...trying to manipulate and control circumstances to our desired outcome. Then, when it doesn't go our way we get angry. The Bible warns us "Be angry but don't sin. Don't give the devil a foothold." (Ephesians 4:32)

Sometimes our anger becomes depression. We medicate with inappropriate things and try to numb the frustration of waiting. We drink ourselves into unconsciousness, or over-medicate with drugs or uncontrolled spending or inappropriate expressions of sex. Anything seems preferable to waiting.

Others wait with resignation. We just quit. I counseled a young military veteran once while I was in Dubai who, just days before, had accidentally run over a Pakistani boy in his Ford F-350 armored vehicle and almost started a riot in the city where he served. It was the father who saved him. The ten-year-old Muslim boy's father came running onto the scene and saw his sons body trapped lifelessly beneath the vehicle. He then looked at the driver and waved his hands saying, "N' Challah...N' Challah.." meaning, "It is the will of Allah." Sometimes we simply resign ourselves under the pressure of "it's God's will so grit your teeth bear it." Islam and some other religious view such resignation as righteousness.

We Should Wait Expectantly

"I waited patiently for the Lord...." the Psalmist testified (Psalm 40:1) The experience of illness or of caring for one who is ill is a graduate school in learning patience. You are forced into it, both patient and caregiver. The physical limitations that my wife experienced following her second brain surgery (an emergency surgery that took place on the same day) radically altered the speed, the focus, and the priority of both of our lives.

From being in the thick of the action we were now firmly located on the sidelines as spectators. From thinking we may have to deal for a few weeks with Pam unable to walk and use her arm as she recuperated, we found ourselves in three weeks of inpatient (or as we jokingly called it, "impatient") rehabilitative therapy. The prognosis we faced revealed that it would take at least three more months before we would even know if it was possible for the nerve function to return to her arm, hand, leg and foot. And as her husband and caregiver I had to wait as well.

We wait. But I have preached (and now I am learning again) that waiting itself is an art. We wait in hope *upon the Lord*. The focus of our waiting must be in the right place. It must, in fact, be on the right person. Waiting patiently means we are trusting the character of the one for whom we are waiting....we trust His word...His promises. "Those who wait *upon the Lord* will renew their strength...." (Isaiah 40:31). We quoted that to ourselves often.

Waiting is also about learning humility. The next time you are in a doctor's office waiting for an appointment (or waiting to go back into the *smaller* waiting room to wait some more), watch who fidgets and gets anxious and angry. It is always the people who feel their rights are being violated and their time hijacked by the doctor's delay. Their "rights" to speedy treatment have been violated! When we are waiting upon the Lord and He has delayed His answer, or His deliverance, or His Presence it seems, our humility or lack thereof comes to the surface quickly.

We Must Wait Confidently

I remembered reading a number of years ago about an earthquake in the Czech Republic in which an elementary school had collapsed which was filled with children. A desperate father fought his way through the security line surrounding the rubble and began digging with his bare hands through the rock and glass and dirt and debris....at the approximate place where his son had been in class.

Hour after hour of desperate digging, his hands bloodied by the effort now assisted by others, he kept digging. In the dark of night he kept digging. And finally, crying out his son's name, he heard a sound... and then the sound became a voice...and he dug more feverishly.

Finally, he moved a board and saw below a small space where his son and two friends were trapped but alive in their pit filled with broken glass and shattered concrete. And when his son saw his father's face, he looked up and smiled and said, "I knew you'd find me father... .I knew you would! I told my friends that my father is coming to find me and they should not worry...because you promised you would!" (Max Lucado, *God Came Near*)

As that little boy trusted the goodness and love and promise of his earthly father, how much more can we trust the goodness and love and promises of our Heavenly Father? Paul tells us in Romans that we wait for what we do not now see. We wait in hope that "all things are working together for good for those who love Him...." (Romans 8:28-29)

The more I live and seek to grow in grace, the more I realize that I must embrace patience as a discipline. We tend to run from this when, in reality, we should run toward this aspect of Christ-like character.

How's your "wait?" We want to be "heavy lifters" in that category. Every hero of faith in the Bible was characterized by seasons of patient waiting. Our ability to wait well should mark our walk with Jesus. Learning to do so is a tough challenge, but we need to learn to be heavy-"wait-ers." Patience, in reality, is not about a timeline...it's a character trait. It is one of the nine "fruit of the Spirit" outlined in Galatians 5:22-23; those attributes that should characterize the follower of Jesus. Learning patience, however, is not about surviving an event; it is a lifetime process of development from which we never graduate.

The Bible celebrates all of the heroes of faith as people who knew how to wait well. Abraham learned to wait for over 25 years for the fulfillment of God's promise that he would father a child. Moses had to wait in training for 40 years in the wilderness before God fulfilled His promise to deliver His people from bondage. The people of Israel marched seven days around the city of Jericho with nothing happening until the seventh time on the seventh day when the walls fell down. The people of God...the persecuted believers of the 21st century...wait patiently for God to intervene in extraordinary suffering. Hebrews 11 gives us a picture of those who waited patiently by faith.

We wait. Your testing ground may be a chronic illness...or a terminal one. It may be the task of caregiving for a loved one with Alzheimer's or MS or a special needs child. Your test may be waiting out the term of a prison sentence or you may be sitting up reading this, waiting for a child to come home from a broken curfew or from years of wandering as a prodigal. Perhaps you are a spouse awaiting word from your husband or wife on deployment. Waiting is not optional in life. How we behave while waiting is our choice.

Waiting Can Be Intentional

The discipline of waiting on the Lord, which honors Him greatly and practically demonstrates our faith, is the choice to keep ourselves focused expectantly. The Psalmist said while still in the pit, "I waited patiently for the Lord...." That in itself is a challenge. When the circumstances that surround you are hopeless, and there is no light on your path and no certainty in your future, "waiting patiently" is an accomplishment. When your feet are sunk in "miry clay" and the walls are slippery and there is no way out unless someone reaches down and pulls you out, "waiting patiently" is not the first thing we think to do.

But that is exactly what we must do. We do this, first, because it's all we can do. We admit our helplessness to self-extract, to wriggle out of this tight space. We stop making every effort to remove ourselves. And we then finally focus our energy on the only One Who can accomplish a Divine rescue. We wait for Him.

Let me clarify this. Waiting is not passivity nor hopeless resignation. We explored every possible option in addressing the diagnosis of glioblastoma. Pam was a twenty-five year veteran of the Mayo Clinic surgical team. We pulled every string, spared no expense, and found ourselves in the care of the best brain surgeon they had. We met with radiologists and were prepared to go forward with follow-up treatments to prolong her life when the door to that option was suddenly slammed shut. They told us, in simple terminology, that her tumor pathology was aggressive, advanced and the worst case scenario...and age was also not in her favor.

We were in the pit....again. Surgery was not the hope we wanted. Due to a genetic issue in the tumor's pathology, chemo and radiation would not produce the desired result but in fact would worsen her quality of life...affecting mobility and cognitive function...with a trade-off of only a few more months of life. We decided that God alone was our Great Physician and Deliverer. He knew the address of the pit we were occupying. We knew once again that we could not pull ourselves out of this, and that no one but God could.

And so we waited. We waited for His Hand to pull us back to the light and life again-back to solid rock and out of the slippery mire we were in. We entrusted ourselves to the care of God's people and prayer, trusting this to be pleasing to God. And we continued to wait patiently....expectantly....confidently...for God's salvation and grace.

CHAPTER 3:

TRUSTING GOD IN THE HARD PLACES

"He inclined to me and heard my cry..."
—Psalm 40:3

I remember growing up in eastern Kentucky and on occasion running in to some folks who were "turned strange." That was Appalachian- American for "they're different than me."
People who were "turned strange" didn't do things or think like the rest of us normal folks. They dipped their French fries in mayonnaise, or preferred grilled chicken to fried. The Nazarenes folks were "turned strange," at least in the mind a boy steeped in deep- fried Southern Baptist churches. But alas, I had broken ranks and chased after a young lady who attended one of these odd and mysterious churches. It was there that I first heard a phrase from the pulpit I had never heard before: "Praying through."

Now the Nazarene folk did enjoy their prayer lives. In every service the altar call had everyone (except me) in the church on their knees....praying. Out loud. Not murmuring, mind you. Not just speaking normally. Shouting. Some were beating their chest or pounding the platform with their hands. The preacher out -prayed them all, but that may not have been faith....that was the microphone. It was chaotic, and even a little scary to an adolescent Baptist boy who had never strayed far from the front yard. Frankly I never went forward in the service because I had no idea what might happen to me if I did!

The strangest thing to me was the people who, after most of the folks went back to their seats and started gathering their belongings and leaving, remained at the altar still praying. Out loud. Together. Sometimes they would gather around one person and pray. It was memorable, I'll give it that, and something I'd never seen in my childhood religious experiences.

But the teenaged girl I was sweet on at that time explained to me, as her parents drove me home, that "praying through" meant you didn't leave the church house or the altar until you were certain you got your answer. She explained that sometimes they would stay more than an hour after the service, "praying through." I left thankful my parents weren't Nazarenes. But I also learned later that their practice was linked to their theology and understanding of "fervent prayer."

I have found myself over the years pondering that odd experience. I have thought about it when sitting in a service with a particularly long Wednesday night prayer meeting and yearned, at least momentarily, for the excitement the Nazarenes had. I have often taught that, if your prayers are boring to you, might they seem the same to God? But more practically, I have thought as a pastor about the phrase "praying through."

When was the last time something moved within you so deeply that you could not stop praying about it? Something that touched you on such a visceral, gut-level that perhaps you even wept? Have you ever had a burden so heavy and so crushing that you could not leave or sleep until you prayed about the person or the need? And you felt compelled to "pray without ceasing?"

Our experience in the hard place of brain cancer drove me and Pam to our knees crying out to God more than anything we'd ever known. Like many believers, Pam and I had always had a very committed individual devotional life, though finding the time to be right for us to do devotions together had been less than consistent. We had always promised ourselves that, when we retired, we would address that. She was faithful in journaling, filled up numerous notebooks over the years. I found out a while back that she would sit and journal through the second service in our church, and all the while I thought my sermons were so good that she wanted to hear them again!

AS I began to realize in the week or so following surgery, and as Pam began to emerge from the influence of some of the medications necessary in the days after, she would not be able to do any devotional reading on a personal level if I did not do that for her. And so, we began a consistent, organized and sometimes (well, I am a pastor) lengthy devotion, culminating in prayer.

We prayed. We prayed for the day-to-day, moment-to-moment issues of pain management, tolerance of the medications she had to take, success in rehab, and the ability to stand/walk/move again with her right side. We prayed for the staff caring for her and in gratitude for the church that was caring for us. We prayed for protection from seizures, and that the surgery had removed most of the tumor and that it would maybe turn out to be non- malignant after all. And we prayed that God would either remove or grant wisdom in knowing what to do with the remainder of the cancer. We prayed about everything. We tried to give thanks in everything. (Philippians 4:6-7) We trusted that our God is a good, good Father and believed in His care. We "waited patiently for the Lord." Desperately hoping as we did so.

And we cried out to Him. We placed our hope, not in changing outer circumstances, but in the unchanging character and nature of our God. We prayed for miraculous, instantaneous healing and recovery. We prayed that our presence would be a testimony for God's glory. WE prayed for endurance, and perseverance, and joy in the midst of the journey.

One day Pam began having consistent, persistent and painful

migraines. They started coming repeatedly. We got one under control, and another started. And another. Twelve all together. That evening our daughter Allison posted that "Mom needs prayer. Now!" Over a hundred people signed on within minutes agreeing in prayer with us. And the migraines stopped!

The next day, we awoke with some anticipation and she had another. It was then our neurologist came into the room, and said, "You're having problems with migraines?" He then told us that he was the lead clinical researcher in the area of migraine treatment related to brain surgery. He gave a couple of suggestions and started her on an over the counter medication.

She never had another one. Coincidence? Or an answer to prayer? WE, of course, did not believe in coincidence.

Crying Out from the Pit

It seems a bit obvious to point out, but one of the continual prescriptions in the Bible when you are in the pit is simply this: Cry out. One author accurately points out that "crying out" in prayer is the most common form of prayer in the Bible, particularly in the Old Testament. There is very little written about "silent prayers" or "moments of silence." Little is said of "keeping your prayer life to yourself." The Bible knows nothing of privatized religion, even if your religious practice got you arrested or otherwise persecuted. Daniel could have avoided a night with the lions if he would have just learned the art of silent prayer!

Let me clarify that last statement. Jesus said, "Do not do your prayers to be seen of men." He never said "go in to your closet/prayer room/private place" and be quiet. He just said shut your door and pray to your Father and don't pray to show off!

It is apparent, even in a brief review, that praying out loud is the preferred manner of prayer recommended in the Bible. When Jesus prayed His most agonizing prayer in the Garden of Gethsemane, and sweat "great drops of blood" as He did so, He cried out loud. "Father, let this cup pass from Me...nevertheless, not My will but Yours be done." The Bible tells us that "In the days of His flesh, He offered up both prayers and supplications with loud crying and tears to the One Who was able to save Him from death." (Hebrews 4:7)

I've never had a problem with public prayer or praying out loud in front of others. But my preferred prayers are those time when I'm alone. And although we have to watch our motives for praying as we do this, God seems to look favorably on those who are willing to make a little noise when they pray.

For years, I had the discipline of rising early to pray (still do) but gradually those prayers became less verbal and more contemplative and quiet. I am, by temperament, an off-the- scale introvert. I'm fine keeping things to myself and just being still.

The church I pastored in Kentucky was on the same exit leading to Gethsemane Monastery in Bardstown. I always wanted to go and just spend some days in solitude and silence with the Trappist monks. Pam told me often I'd make a great monk, thought I'm not sure if she was complimenting me or not!

When we entered our trial with cancer, my mental/emotional/spiritual life was turned upside down. I was disoriented internally. The thoughts were coming jumbled and sometimes I could not organize or finish a sentence. For a brief time, though I knew God was never absent, it felt as though God was absent. I lost my prayer life....or so I thought.

And I panicked. It was then God brought to my mind the reality that, when you're in the pit, you don't whisper to get out. You don't mumble. You yell. You scream out loud.

You cry out to Jesus. Pain makes us scream. When I'm sitting in the dentist's chair and the procedure is causing pain, I find a way to "cry out" even with a mouthful of metal and plastic. When we break a bone, we don't sit in pain silently thinking to ourselves, "wow this hurts." We cry out.

IN one of our prayer times together, God brought to mind the story of Peter walking on water. It seemed to connect with our experience on several levels. But Scripture reminded that, when Peter sank, he didn't "take a moment of silence." He cried out! "Lord, save!" And the Lord heard and saved him. I wonder sometimes what would have happened to Peter if he HADN'T cried out. And more than that, I sometimes wonder what happens to us because we won't cry out when we're sinking as Peter was.

One of the major influences in my early Christian walk was a young musician from Brooklyn named Keith Green. Keith wrote songs that were more sermons than lyrical. And in his concerts, he often preached between the songs. In one prayer chorus he wrote these words:

> *My eyes are dry*
> *My faith is old*
> *My heart is hard*
> *My prayers are cold...*
> *"My Eyes are Dry"*
> —Keith Green

I listened to these words in the early days of my Christian walk when praying seemed less difficult and life was simpler. My prayer life was fine in those early days, and growing deeper. But life....cancer, depression, or just life in general....has a way of testing that. Our prayers can grow cold. Our hearts can become hard. And our eyes no longer shed tears of joy or of repentance. We lose our fervency in prayer. It has happened to me more times than I care to recount.

I began to realize that something had to happen or I was going to tumble deeper into this pit. When you are in this position as many have been before us you learn that the battle you are fighting is coming on several fronts: physical, mental, emotional, and spiritual. I had to find my voice before God again....I had to cry out to Him for mercy. I felt I was losing all the other battles at the moment, but was determined not to lose the spiritual one. Too much was at stake for me to stumble at this point now.

And so that day, I took a walk. I talked to God. I shouted. I wept. And I learned I hadn't lost my prayer life at all....in fact I had found my voice before God at a much deeper level.

Prayer essentially is making time to talk to God...and allowing time for Him to talk to us. Now please understand that I am not prescribing for you what you must do with this. I am simply giving testimony of what happened to me. I learned there are seasons when our "sweet hour of prayer" is not to be spent in solitude and silence surrounded by roses. Sometimes our prayers are shouted with tears and sweat and accompanied by blood and desperation and, on occasion, answered with silence.

But I was also reminded through this ordeal that my prayer life didn't cease just because I couldn't find the words. God gives us the words. Many nights during rehab, lying awake on the sofa beside Pam's bed, unable to sleep for the beeps and blinking lights of nearby medical equipment and noisy people in the hallway, I was praying. I never once believed God left us in all of this....and neither did she.

We have been prayed over several times....both in person and, I have been assured, many times without being present. Our church took time on several occasions and with hot tears and outpouring of emotion, prayed for Pam's recovery and healing. Our deacons laid hands on Pam (and me), anointed her with oil as the Bible commands, and prayed for her to be healed. It was a sweet and faith-filled time, both with the church and with the deacons.

If the sheer number of people who have been praying for Pam's recovery that I was aware of and the many, many folks who I'm sure I was not aware of, mattered most to God then her healing would be assured. We had, to my knowledge, seven different language groups around the world praying for her....including Haiti, Cuba, Romania and the Philippines, Even a group in Iraq had been praying for her!

I learned that a group of inmates from Tomoka prison near Daytona held a 24 hour prayer vigil for her. (I have since learned two other prison groups had also been praying). On the day I learned about Tomoka's inmates, I spoke to the Sheriff of St John's County, Florida who told me that the staff and officers at the Sheriff's office who are believers had been praying for her. Countless churches from all across the country and various denominations had been praying. The Executive Committee of the Southern Baptist Convention, meeting in Phoenix in 2017, stopped their proceedings to lift her up in prayer. I can add more, but you get the point. If sheer force of numbers was all it took to turn the hand and heart and Sovereignty of Almighty God, then we had this...at least as far as the math was concerned.

Sheer numbers of people, however, are not what impresses God. He is looking for faith "the size of a grain of mustard seed." Did we have that?

Praying through, as my Nazarene neighbors called it, has a dimension of desperation...or "fervency" involved in it. The "effectual, fervent prayer of a righteous man avails much" we read in the Book of James. I preached once on the importance of not stopping one prayer short of the answer that God is going to give.

That particular Sunday as I spoke on not giving up too quickly in prayer, an Indian family in our church listened. They had tried desperately time and again to adopt a little girl from their home country, but every door seemed shut in their face. Finally, they just gave up. Then they heard the challenge to pray one more time. They did, and that time doors started opening in amazing ways. Sometimes God just wants us not to quit.

We are to "keep on asking, keep on seeking, and keep on knocking." We are to be like the widow before the unrighteous judge, continually petitioning him for justice. We are to imitate the desperate friend who awoke his neighbor for bread in the middle of the night. I have been that persistent widow and that annoying neighbor to God many times through this trial. I have often preached these ideas and images and truths. Practicing them, however, takes a discipline beyond the ordinary.

DA Carson, who has written several remarkable theological works, wrote a book on prayer in the early 1990's entitled *Praying with Paul.* In that book, he suggested the following practical steps to praying effectively. It is, arguably, the greatest need in the church as well as in every Christian's life. I offer an adaptation to his suggestions here:

1. *Plan to pray.* We know we should. We agree that we should. And yet, much does not happen in prayer because we have not planned to do it. Schedule it. Prioritize it. We don't pray much because we don't actually plan to do it, choosing instead to "find" some time in our day if it works out. It probably won't.
2. *Avoid mental distraction.* Now that seems to be an impossible task for some. All of us are "wired" with different temperaments, and prayer is incredibly flexible. Some prefer to find a place of solitude and quiet to shut out distractions. Others would rather pray "on the fly" as they drive to work or walk or pace as they pray. Some prefer silence and reflection, while others need praise music and the opportunity to pray out loud. It doesn't matter. But praying without distraction is a necessity for a growing prayer experience. Our minds are wired to be distracted, and our culture obliges with hundreds of ways to distract. Focus your attention by reading Scripture first. Others benefit from journaling prayers and requests. What works best for you is the best approach...but intentionally work to avoid mental "drift."
3. *Develop prayer relationships.* Have a prayer partner if at all possible. This needs to be a person of the same sex, since true intimacy in prayer can unintentionally lead to intimacy in other

areas. This person needs to be an individual you can trust not to be a gossip. If you are married seek to develop a prayer relationship with your spouse as one aspect of this. If you have children, schedules can conflict and complicate. But planning even an evening a week to meet as a family to read Scripture, pray, and sing together can deeply impact everyone involved.

4. *Find good models.* We learn to pray in the same way we learn to talk...by imitation. If you are a consistent prayer, you can no doubt look back and find someone who influenced you to do that. Every prayer model is not a good model, so when you choose to imitate the prayers and prayer lives of others make sure they are good models. If you are a parent, you need to be aware that you will most likely be the first model of the importance of prayer. Even if you are not meeting regularly with the children to pray, be aware they are watching even when you think they aren't. Be a good model, and find a model living or dead, to follow.

5. *Mingle intercession with praise and confession.* As much as possible, learn to tie your requests and intercession to Scripture. Paul models this for us in numerous places in the New Testament. We acknowledge the Sovereignty of God in prayer, but that does not dismiss us from the responsibility of interceding for others, even believing "The Lord is God; He does whatever He will." Neither should we shoulder a burden that says that "it's all up to me and my prayer life." One of the hardest lessons I learned in passing through our trial was that "prayer does not change things." And we cannot beat down the doors of Heaven by bombarding Him with what we want. We stand somewhere between those two extremes in our prayer lives, but it is God's desire for us to intercede. "The Spirit gives us utterance...." and that means that the God Who prompts you to prayer will help you to know how to pray according to His will. And we continue

praying, whether it accomplishes our will or not.

6. *Pray until you pray.* The old Quaker movement and Puritan groups used to cite this often. How long should we pray? Until we have prayed. When do we know we're done? When we've prayed! When we've moved past the unreality and formalism that characterizes much of our prayers. No wonder we tire so easily...sometimes we quit before we have even entered into the Presence of God! When you have tasted of the Father's Presence, even for a moment, you will long for more and more. This becomes the driving force of our prayer life. We need to think of prayer less like a 140 word Twitter post and more like singing a love song to our Beloved.

I will add one more thing to Dr Carson's excellent list. We need to pray as a means of achieving a relationship more than receiving an answer. When my daughter or son call me "just to talk," it is my delight as a father. They called just because they like me, or enjoy a few moments in my presence. I am no less delighted when they call needing something, and it thrills me to be allowed to give what they ask. However, the joy in my heart when they just want to "hang out" with me for a few moments far outweighs them coming to me because they need something.

I cannot help but think that our Heavenly Father just longs to hear from His children just because they delight in Him as their Father, and not because He has something in His hand that they want. This requires us to dig deep into our own heart to determine the motivation of our prayer life. And so we prayed until we prayed. We wept with fervency. And we waited patiently for God's deliverance to come.

CHAPTER 4:

A SHATTERED VESSEL

If ever the resume of a person suffering for the name of Jesus was put into print, we find it in the identity of the Apostle Paul. His influence has been so great that it has led some to credit him as the "founder" of Christianity! While that claim is not correct, Paul's writings have shaped much of Christian thought for almost two millennia and his life follows the contour of a path of hardship and struggle as he walked with the risen Christ. In fact, his calling and conversion (which happened simultaneously) contained a promise in the Book of Acts that he would suffer much for the sake of Jesus' name.

At the center of a life that lays out the price paid by this one "born out of time," Paul speaks of the experience that comes to any and all who would be followers of the Lamb. While there is abounding joy and abundant peace, there will also come times of difficulty, stress, and suffering. Unlike the theology peddled by some today who promote that Christians will experience ease, wealth, and success, Paul tells the follower of Christ to expect affliction, suffering, and persecution for the sake of their Lord.

If we don't grasp this then when unexpected illness, or a job loss, or the death of a family member comes it will throw us into a tailspin of despair. When we embrace the reality of crucifixion and the dying of our flesh, and see it as resulting in glory and not just a cosmic mistake or bad karma, we will grow and not wither. The "weight of glory" will far outweigh our "light and momentary afflictions." (2 Corinthians 4:17) While God does discipline those He loves when their lives fall out of alignment with Him (Hebrews 12:1-4), often our suffering seems to us to have no rhyme or reason.

Within a scant few hours of my wife's final breath on earth, I wrote these words for a blog I never completed before she died:

THE GLORY TO BE REVEALED

I write these words late in the evening. Darkness has fallen, literally and figuratively. Just a few feet from me, lying in our bed, is my wife. She has struggled now for almost 48 hours with the final steps of life before her transition from physical struggle to spiritual glory.

As I listen to her ragged breathing, I am trying to remember what I learned long ago and teach every time I meet with someone who is hurting. For the Christian, this life...however rough the road may be....leads to eternal, wondrous glory. "We look not at the things which are seen...but the things which are not seen. For the things that we can now see are temporary...the things we cannot see are eternal." (2 Corinthians 4:14-15)

I have meditated often on those words over the last 3 1/2 months. From the perspective of humanity, and we all live in that and default to that view, there is nothing glorious about a brain tumor or the ravages it leaves in its wake. To see cancer, or other illness or those things in life which ultimately break us then shape us, from a human vantage point is to see nothing but loss...nothing but tragedy. Nothing but pain. Nothing but injury and loss of dignity. And nothing....nothing of hope.

To look at cancer or other struggles in life from the "ground up" is to lose a very important perspective on life; namely...this present life is not all there is. There is something greater, something more

lasting, something more glorious than we could ever imagine await-
ing us. "It has not entered into the heart of man the things that God
has prepared for those who love Him."

Hours after this was written, my bride entered victoriously into
the reality of that wonderful truth. She saw face-to-face the One Who
had prepared this for her and carried her from her death bed to the reality of that glory.

Moving from the crushing and bruising experiences of life to
seeing them as glory now requires a radical change in perspective and
a firm grasp on our faith. We cannot look at pain and suffering in our
lives or in that of others as anything but tragic without it.

But when we see our struggle in the bright light of the resurrection, then we can see that none of it is wasted. None of it. Not one tear.
Does that mean that the chemotherapy doesn't make you sick or sitting
outside in the hallway of a courtroom awaiting the verdict concerning
one of your children doesn't break your heart? Pain is still painful. Disappointment still saddens. Tears are still salty and wet.

Paul never promised or provided an escape route from our pain.
He simply pointed out, as God inspired his words, that having the right
perspective on our pain frames it in meaning beyond the hurt. I reminded myself and my wife of this often during our journey through
terminal cancer. We still hurt. We still wept. We still lost sleep. We still
were sorrowful.

But we also knew that glory lay beyond this...and that somehow
in ways we did not now understand God was bringing that glory about
in her life and mine. We clung desperately to the promise that "in all
these things God is working," bringing our good and His glory even in
the crushing experience we were going through.

We read in 2 Corinthians 4-5 the centerpiece of Paul's explanation of why suffering comes. While some suffering has a direct correla-
tion to disobedience and discipline, (and even in that "it is good that

we were afflicted" according to the Psalmist, I am thinking more directly here about suffering that comes even to those who are walking closely with God. Obviously, Paul's experience shows that the most devout follower of Christ will find pain on the pathway home.

He reminds us that we have "this treasure in earthen vessels." "Jars of clay" is an accurate rendering. Clay pots. We are a few dollars and a few cents worth of minerals and dirt at the end of the day. Enough phosphorus to ignite a matchstick and a few other assorted chemicals left over. The rest is fluid. Just water and dirt. Mud. Clay.

The most common vessel in a Middle Eastern or Mediterranean household of the day was a clay pot...mud and water. There were few metal utensils. And, believe it or not, no Tupperware! Just clay. Fragile. Perishable. Easily broken. Often cracked.

My son Dave is my pottery "specialist." He teaches 3D art and loves pottery making; throwing wet clay on a wheel, shaping a piece, and then firing it in a kiln. I've learned more about pottery from him than I knew there was to know. And I have learned that the firing of the newly-formed product is very important.

There is a proper temperature and a proper time that the item is to be left in the kiln. Too little time and heat, and the pot won't harden. Too much, and it becomes brittle and cracks appear. The potter knows just how long and how much heat is necessary not to remove it from the kiln too early or leave it too long. If the pottery you are making is intended to carry water or other liquids, cracks are a problem.

But these pots were used, not only for water storage and cooking and cleaning; they were also used to house precious treasures and to be a place for candles to light the home. As a place to store treasure or as a housing for light, a cracked vessel may not present a problem.

The law of gravity proves this: If there is a way for liquid to escape a vessel, it's going to do so. If your vessel is broken or cracked, the liquid within will spill out; usually at the most inconvenient moment! Reality teaches us that what is inside of us will come out eventually. There are no permanently sealed vessels.

Middle Eastern artisans of the day would sometimes try to hide the less noticeable cracks in their vessels by coating them with wax. The wax would seal for a time, but eventually what was inside would leak through. This practice required honest artisans to place a notice on their tables as they sold their wares: "sine cera..without wax."

Of course we still use those words today every time we speak of being "sincere." We are saying "what you see is what you get." No wax. Nothing hidden. Though we may try we cannot forever hide the cracks!

When life "cracks" your vessel, and mistreatment or hardship or difficulty comes, what is inside your "vessel" will escape. This is why we are reminded in the Bible to "be filled with the Spirit," so when times of testing come the Spirit is what will spill out of you.

But if you are filled with something else, that ALSO will come out in times of difficulty.Something is going to shatter your vessel. In fact, it is true to say we are all "cracked pots." And it is equally true that, as a believer in Christ, you "contain" the ultimate treasure that IS Christ. It is "Christ in you, the hope of glory." (Colossians 1:27)

Jesus, Who claimed to be the "light of the world," has chosen to reside in you and more than that, to shine gloriously through you! How does He do that? Through the cracks!

The light comes through the broken places.It is "through our weakness that His strength is perfected," Paul will tell us later in this incredible letter.

So in reality, the bigger the cracks, the more the light escapes! The weaker we become in our physical person the more radically His power is seen through us. The more we feel physically limited and dependent upon Him, the more God has opportunity to, if you would, "slip out" through the cracks in our "jar." The more we decrease, the more He can increase in us.

In Paul's experience, and in ours, some things are commonplace. He mentions in 2 Corinthians 4:13 that he has been "hard pressed" on every side. That simply means he found himself "between a rock and a hard place." No way out. He was pressed beyond measure, but "not crushed." Like the people of Israel in the formation of their identity as a people, Paul found himself in impossible situations doing business with a God Who does impossible things. The only way the people of Israel escaped the clutches of Pharoah or death on the shore of the Red Sea was by God parting the sea so they could cross, not only unharmed but even without muddy sandals!

He adds that he has often been "perplexed." Paul was a smart man. A trained rabbi. A legal scholar. A "Pharisee among Pharisees." He knew his stuff. But he found himself in circumstances that had no logical purpose. He had questions. He was perplexed.

Maybe you've been there. Often a person unacquainted with the Bible or seeking to disprove the existence of a loving God, will ask "If there is a God, why do bad things happen to innocent people?" Now I know what they're after when they ask this question. But if you know what the Bible teaches you know, first of all, that there have only been two people born innocent. One of those lost their innocence in the Garden of Eden, and therefore "by one man, sin entered" all mankind. Only one innocent person has ever been born and remained innocent- the Lord Jesus Christ.

And when He suffered crucifixion, and the humiliation, and torture and pain and sin-bearing on the cross, He experienced suffering like no other human being. Jesus, the most innocent, also endured the most pain. And by that one man "salvation came to all."

But in that excruciating cross-experience, the glory of God was most clearly seen. Even in that, His flesh cried out "My God, my God why have You forsaken Me?" He was, as Paul said, "perplexed." Now, you may ask, "if Jesus was God as Christians claim, how could He have questions?" Because He was also as much human as He was Deity. Not half-and-half, but fully human and fully Deity.

But sometimes, our humanity reaches out with questions. "Why do bad things happen?" As I write this a massive hurricane recently ripped through the southern United States and another through the islands of the Caribbean. They destroyed bars and houses of prostitution and meth labs as well as houses of worship. Criminal and Christ-followers alike lost homes and possessions. Bad things happen...to everyone. And in the wake of those times, questions often linger.

I would be less than honest if I did not say that Pam and I were" perplexed" about her cancer diagnosis. We asked hard questions addressed to our medical team, to those who had walked similar paths, of ourselves and to God. Many of these questions will remain unanswered until I stand in God's Presence, as she does now. We ask questions that are intellectual in nature and framed through the experience of our limited flesh.

But in reality we learned that the answers to some of the questions we were asking were too deep for us to receive. God's ways are in fact, higher than our ways, and His thoughts higher than our thoughts. (Isaiah 55:8-9) And so although she now knows fully, I will continue to trust a good, good Father that what He does is best.

Beyond that, however, is this fact. If we were able to comprehend God's answers to the questions we have, they would still not fix the problem. Our pain is not caused by our intellectual confusion. It is rooted in our emotion. A "head" answer is not going to fix a "heart" issue. It is, at the end of the day, a matter of faith to simply trust God with it.

Paul also said "we are not in despair." In others words, the believer will have faith that, even if they do not possess the answer to the question "why," we have faith that God does and that He is working "all things together for the good of those who love Him." That knowledge keeps us from falling into despair.

In the same verses, he said "we are persecuted..." That's a word that's easy to misread. We think we know what it means. But as American Christians, we are far from knowing what persecution really means.

According to missiologist Dr Nik Ripken, persecution takes place whenever the enemy attempts to silence and shut out the testimony of the believer about Jesus. In earlier days, believers would have their tongues cut out before being burned alive or thrown to wild beasts because they would continue singing and praising God, even to their deaths. "They overcame by the blood of the Lamb and the word of their testimony and they loved not their lives to the death." Men had tried to silence Paul's testimony to the risen Lord Jesus. They had beaten him with rods, with whips, stoned him, and thrown him into prison, all in an effort to keep him from talking about Jesus.

In times when people turn against you or when legal authorities come and take you away in the middle of the night, as is true in some parts of the world such as China today, you find out quickly who will stand with you...and who won't. Loneliness becomes a terrible form of persecution in itself as the enemy uses it to torment you further.

But Paul said, "we were persecuted, but not abandoned." They knew, as did the three Hebrew men named Shadrach, Meshach and Abednego in the Book of Daniel that, even in the flames of persecution they were not alone. There was "a fourth man in the fire" with them. Paul knew that, even though all had forsaken him, God would not.

And finally he said, "we are knocked down, but not knocked out." He is the fighter who keeps getting up even though bloodied and broken. He is the soldier who walks into gunfire against overwhelming odds, or the first responder who runs into the crisis when everyone else is trying to get out. He is the cancer patient who gets up to take one more round of radiation or chemotherapy. He is the discouraged pastor who shows up one more time to bring the Word of God to people. He is the Mom who won't give up on her wayward son or daughter.

I've always loved the Rocky movies. They're pretty much all the same and are not exactly the high point of cinematic art, but I have watched all of them. And every one ends the same way. Rocky gets knocked down. Then, he gets back up...bloodied, bruised, looking defeated...and then he comes back and wins. He is the icon of endurance under pressure for many.

This is you, when you refuse to surrender to the pressures around you to compromise or even abandon the faith. He is you, when you realize that the sufferings of this present time are not worthy to be compared to the glory to be revealed." He is you when you decide that you will not lose heart, even though everything in your circumstances and every voice around you tells you that you should.

The glory of God is that which we should most seek, no matter the stage or circumstance of our life. Nothing is worth more. And nothing costs more. But unlike every valuable thing that seems priceless on this earth, it is something that will last eternally. In 10,000 years, your suffering, your tears, and your scars will still matter. And the weight of God's glory will still shine through you.

But to get there, our clay must first be shattered. Our flesh must be crushed. Our dependence must be upon God and not our own resources. And then...His glory will fill us. Our light will shine through in a dark world.

And whatever price we are called to pay, it will not be worth comparing to the glory that will be revealed. For that glory we hope... and for His glory we live. For then and only then will our temporary loss will become eternal gain!

CHAPTER 5:

SEEING FROM HEAVEN'S VIEW

So much of our experience hinges on perspective, especially our understanding of suffering and trials. A few years ago, my son and I went on a night patrol with a helicopter crew from the Jacksonville Sheriffs Office. From hundreds of feet in the air, the city of Jacksonville sparkled like a diamond in the night. It looked much different than the view of the city from my car windshield when I'm stalled in rush hour or construction traffic. Same city. Same roads. Different perspective.

When we view the trials and difficulties of life from a heavenly perspective we see a different reality than the view "on the ground." During high school I used to dread marching band season. I loved music, and really liked the band. But I played sousaphone...a brass instrument that seemed to weigh 150 pounds...and I weighed 145.

I still remember the first time I saw a videotaped, press box perspective of our award-winning show. I saw the formations. I saw the precision. I saw myself and the other five tuba players in the band. And when I saw it, I got it. Perspective changed my attitude. The tuba was no lighter...but now I knew why I was carrying it.

A while back I went to my first NASCAR event in Bristol. I'm not a fan, truth be told. But I went with a friend, and was treated to a suite at the very top of the track where we stayed through much of the early part of the race. It was like watching it on a really large-screen TV in air-conditioned comfort.

But one of my friends suggested toward the end of the race that we go down to the track. I thought he meant "go sit on the bleachers." He meant "go to the track." We got on ground level where the cars were flying past only a few feet away from us, separated only by a chain-link fence. As we stayed there through ten laps, and the speed of the cars literally thumped my chest as they passed, I came away picking black pieces of rubber tire from my hair....and I got it. The difference was staggering. My perspective changed.

Getting a God's-eye view of our pain and problems is essential if we are not going to lose heart when they come. Several books "assisted" me on my journey of caregiving in Pam's final months. One in particular gripped me and would not let me go. Written by author T.W. Hunt after the death of his wife from breast cancer and co-written by his daughter who was at that time also going through breast cancer, the book is entitled *From Heaven's View*. It helped me time and time again not to remain focused on what we were seeing or experiencing from a human vantage point, but to try and see it as God saw it.

Each of the inspired writers of the New Testament bring a "heavenly perspective" to our struggles and problems. James reminds us in the opening few words of his letter to "consider it all joy" (James 1:1-2) when we enter trials and temptations. Peter reminds us that "the fiery trial" we are enduring is designed, not to consume us but to purify and prepare us for an eternal purpose.

Paul reminds us to do the same thing in the closing verses of 2 Corinthians 4. There we read "though our outer man perishes, yet the inner man is being renewed day by day.

"The things that are seen are temporary, but the things that are not seen are eternal." This is seeing from Heaven's view. It is the "press box perspective"on the field. It is the ability to see our trials transformed into eternal gold. To see our pain process through as joy. To allow our sorrows and struggles to work into us hope and endurance, faith and patience.

These things can come in no other way. But they require a fundamental shift in our understanding of God's purpose in our life. We need to see from Heaven's view.

First, we must understand that, from God's perspective, eternity is more important than time. If you'll take a piece of paper and draw a line all the way across, and then with the point of your pencil or pen, add a pinpoint dot anywhere on the line, you can visualize the contrast of eternity with your life. Your life is the do. Eternity begins before the page and continues after the page. We are time-bound creatures. We live from day-to-day, season to season, month to month.

This is the "box" that God created for us to exist in. And we are bound to it. We order our lives around it. Go for a day and try not to look at your watch, or your phone to see what time it is. We are time-conscious, and for a reason: To remind us that our days are limited, but something beyond time awaits.

But God is not time-bound. He lives from an eternal vantage point. There are no clocks in Heaven. No watches. No calendars. In Heaven, it is always NOW. So God sees life, not as our slowly slogging through our days and muddling through our months. He sees the end and the beginning. "A day with the Lord is as a thousand years, and a thousand years as a day" we are reminded in 2 Peter. Seventy or ninety years may seem a long time to us unless we have lived them, and then we say "it happened so fast!" The dot really is brief.

I remember a little story I heard a few years ago about a turtle being mugged by a snail. When the turtle was asked later for a description of the snail, he said, "I don't remember what he looked like. It all happened so fast." Time, as Einstein would later theorize, is relative.

God is doing an eternal, though unseen work in each of His children. Though this work is done in different ways, it is always done with an eternal value in mind. This helps us when we or someone we love is hurting. Seeing the end result makes whatever we must endure worth it in eternity.

Second, from Heaven's view, the purpose of our life is not to be happy. It is not simply to live a contented and satisfying life on this temporary planet. God's purpose is our transformation into the likeness of Jesus Christ. For all of our disagreements about predestination, I hear very few argue this verse: "For God has predestined us to be conformed to the image of His Son." (Romans 8: 26)

Since Jesus is the only One Who has pleased God on the earth, the Father desires that we all bear His image. The name "Christian" is used infrequently in the New Testament. In fact for the early followers of "the Way" of Jesus Christ, this term was one of derision and mocking...not honor.

It came about as an unbelieving world began to watch the people who followed Jesus as imitating His way of life. The term "Christian" means "little Christ." The church later embraced the term, not as mocking but as an honorable title. They lived like Jesus. They talked like Jesus. They did business like Jesus.

Nothing pleases the Father more than to see His children, Christ-followers, bearing a likeness to His Son. The best way to make God known to an unbelieving culture is to look like Jesus and to live like Jesus in every way possible. They will never believe us otherwise.

But one of the ways, a hard way at least from our perspective, that God uses to create the image of His Son....to stamp the character of Christ into our life....is through the things we suffer. As Christ suffered for us the death of a criminal, so we are to 'fill up the sufferings' of Christ" in our life. God begins the process of turning every sorrow, every tear into a tool that etches Christ-likeness into us.

We are like a piece of stone in the sculptors hand. When he decides what he wants to shape the stone to be, he begins knocking off pieces of the stone...the pieces that DON'T look like the image he is wanting to create. Now if the stone could speak, it would say "That hurts!" As the hammer and chisel do their work, and pieces of the stone fall away, slowly the image appears. If possible, the stone would stop the artists hand from his work, being content with being a shapeless, formless rock. But as the sculptor works, a work of art is crafted and in the end becomes something useful and even beautiful.

The same process is taking place in your life and mine if we have Christ in us as our Savior. The things of our flesh that hinder our like-ness to Jesus must be taken away, by force and violence if necessary. The pieces of our "stone" that we have become attached to must yield to the Artist's hand if we are to fulfill our greatest purpose and destiny. But this interferes with what we would understand a "happy" life to consist of...one without pain or sorrow or tears.

Third, reflecting the Father's likeness is God's ultimate desire. We arrive at this as the "hope of glory" that is Christ in us is released as our flesh falls away. Doing this requires a daily crucifixion. And it requires a purified faith.

Most of our married life of forty years, Pam and I have either been in school or in ministry. Early on, since I wasn't earning a paycheck, she realized the necessity of not spending a lot of money. So she became interested in garage sales and then became the queen of them. She could find the best stuff in the junk heaps that people were throwing out! Still today, our home is decorated in a late 20th Century Yard Sale motif!

For a period of time, she got interested in collecting old copper kitchenware. She would bring home some of the ugliest pots and pans with a barely recognizable copper bottom. Then, she'd go to work. Scraping, using chemicals, soaking and starting over. And before long, the accumulated tarnish and stains would disappear and a lovely item of kitchen cookware would appear in her hand! In fact, this virtually unusable pot or pan would be shined so perfectly that you could see your face on the bottom! She could see the potential as she shopped.

In much the same way, God takes us and sometimes puts us

through the fire. We have the same problem as the pots and pans. We are tarnished and stained by sin and this distorts the image of God in us. He is determined to return us to the place where we bear His image clearly.

And so He goes to work on us; polishing, and scraping, and placing us in the white-hot flames of affliction. It was a practice of the goldsmiths of Biblical times to heat gold found in the mines to burn away the impurities. As the gold continued to be heated by the flame, it would release the dirt and other contaminates which were always lighter. The gold would sink to the bottom. The impurities remain on the top. When they accumulated enough, the goldsmith would scrape these impurities away and leave only pure gold....gold that was so pure he could see his face in it as though it were a mirror.

You may be in a fiery place today. Peter spoke to early Christians and reminded them that their faith would be tested and purified as "though gold in the fire." As we release the impurities of sin and the dominance of the flesh in our lives, the remaining faith (that which will last for eternity) will reflect the Father's face.

As the cancer in her brain continued to grow and spread, bringing limitations and loss and sorrow and tears in its wake, we struggled. But the times we struggled were the times when our earthly view obstructed the Heavenly one. Sometimes she would have to remind me of that, and other times I reminded her.

Can I say I was always joyful for what we were going through... as I saw my bride of forty years physically and mentally wasting away? I'm afraid not. But in those moments when we both "got it," and we saw the cancer through the lens of the Master Artist doing a work in her "clay pot," the joy would come. As more and more I knew the likeness of Christ was being imprinted in our spirits and even though her outer person was wasting away, we could rejoice.

We learned quickly that as soon as our eyes turned to the temporary, to the physical, the tears of grief would flow. But when we realized that the fire of affliction was both now and eternally forming Christ- in-her, our sorrow would turn to joy.

Not one moment of her pain was a waste. Not one disappoint-ment will be forgotten by the Father. And in the end, though she is "ab-sent from the body," and absent from me for a brief time, I rejoice to know that her "light, momentary afflictions" have worked in her a "far more eternal weight of glory."

And in that last moment as she was able to see her Savior face-to-face, I am confident of this: As He looked at her, He could see His own face looking back at Him.

And He will see it for eternity.

CHAPTER 6:

REDISCOVERING INTIMACY WITH GOD

The men who walked with Jesus had opportunity to see Him do, time and again, incredible and miraculous things. The blind saw. The lame walked. The deaf could hear, the mute could speak. Demons fled. Multitudes were fed. Jesus walked on water. The dead were raised to life.

But there is only one place recorded in the Gospels where they asked Jesus for a tutorial. In Luke 11, they requested that He teach them to pray! Not, "Jesus teach us how to feed people." "Teach us how to heal the sick." "Teach us how to cast out demons." Only this. "Teach us to pray."

Our experience in the hard place threw us into the classroom with the disciples. We wrestled with how to pray....how to ask...what to pray....and sought the face of God in prayer more than we ever had. And we prayed fervently....faithfully...persistently.

But not only that, we also prayed in community. I have never, ever personally known of one person who was prayed for more than my wife was. We knew that literally thousands of believers around the nation...people we never met....were praying. We received hundreds of intricate, handmade angels from a group of ladies from eight different states who sent prayer cards with their handiwork. We received cards from church prayer groups, at least two groups of prisoners in Florida. Catholic, Methodist, Anglican and Baptists alike. Denominations did not seem to eradicate compassion. At last count, believers in seven different countries were praying. Even many children sent cards, and posters and videos telling us they were praying!

If the sheer volume of people approaching the throne for Pam would make any difference, then I felt assurance we had this thing beaten! If persistence was all it took to turn the heart of God to consider healing Pam from the scourge of cancer, then I felt confident we would be ok. If simply asking the Father in faith was what was necessary, He was asked in faith. If being specific was what He wanted, we were specific. If coming in fasting and prayer was what He wanted, we were covered. If being sincere and repentant as best as we could know ourselves, and being selfless mattered, then the answer was around the corner.

Jesus taught His disciples in these verses to "ask, seek, and knock." Elementary Greek teaches that you study the ending of verbs to truly understand how to translate what some words meant. The endings of the verbs translated "ask, seek, and knock" are more accurately understood as "keep asking, keep seeking, and keep knocking."

This we did. We drew near to God in prayer. We did it together, and I assure you I did it alone. I prayed Scripture over her. I claimed verses for her. We listened to God.

And I believe He heard. Truly I do. But He chose not to give us the miracle or the healing we had petitioned from Him. So why do we pray? I have had to rethink and reaffirm what I believe about praying in situations like this. I believe God hears our prayers and answers according to His will and purposes.

Prayer is not about getting what we want from the hand of God. We move too quickly and impatiently in our prayers, wanting to get our needs met, as an anxious child who wants to get money from his parent but doesn't take time to hang out with Mom or Dad. He wants his need met....and wants it now! But God does not design prayer to be a "quick fix" for our discomforts or just speaking a set of "magic words" that tries to manipulate Him to do the trick we want Him to do.

God wants us, in fact, to seek His Face before we seek what's in His hand. He wants to draw us closer in intimacy with Him whether we are standing in the sunshine or shivering in the rain. The pit seems to accelerate our ability to understand God's grace and sufficiency for whatever we might be experiencing. It is a lesson that we would willingly put off to another day if left up to us, as far as our flesh is concerned. Suffering forces us to draw near to God, not for an answer, but for His grace and Presence to sustain us in our pain.

Paul learned this lesson and the Spirit of God inspired him to write about it in 2 Corinthians 12. There we learned that Paul was suffering from a "thorn" in his flesh (the original translation tells us it was, in reality, not a splinter but a "stake," or "tent peg") that tormented him constantly. He prayed three times for this torturous pain (I personally believe he had malaria) to be removed and he heard God's voice tell him, "My grace is sufficient for you." And to our knowledge, God left the thorn in place....but He also left the grace needed to deal with it.

God wants us deepening and drawing near in a relationship with Him. Not a casual, back -slapping superficial kind of friendship but an intimate, daily, moment-by-moment fellowship. In the Garden of Eden, Adam and Eve lost two precious things as a direct result of their sinful choice. They first of all lost intimacy with each other. They had the most amazing, totally transparent relationship two human beings had ever experienced on earth. They understood each other. They were "naked and not ashamed," and had nothing to hide from the other. They didn't fear rejection...who would they reject the other for?

But now, because of sin, there was shame. There was hiding. They knew they were naked, and their self-consciousness of that fact made them run for the bushes to scrape together clothing knit from leaves. Now, they were naked .... and ashamed...and living in the shadows behind their separate "bushes."

Yet they also lost intimacy with God. For the first time since their creation, and we don't know how long that period lasted, they missed their daily "walk" with God. And God came looking for them in the Garden, asking "Adam, where are you?" From behind the bush where he was hiding himself, Adam spoke. God said, "who told you that you were naked?" Adam blamed his wife. She blamed the serpent. And the rest you know is the ugly history of how sin entered the human race. "For as by one man sin entered the human race...." (Romans 5:12)

Returning to intimacy with God and with others is an irreplaceable part of spiritual growth. God continues to ask, "Adam, where are you?" Put your name at the beginning of that question. Where are you? Are you near, or far away from God right now?

I love the ocean. Particularly I love the clear blue waters of Hawaii and the emerald green waters of the Caribbean. I have had the joy of exploring both in my lifetime. I have snorkeled in the Florida Keys and I have gone scuba diving off the coast of Maui in Hawaii. Both experiences were wonderful, but I liked diving the best.

Snorkeling yields it's share of discoveries and joy, and without cumbersome equipment needed to stay under water. You could become "one" with ocean life very quickly by simply putting on mask and fins and breathing with your air hose.

But once I went diving, I never really cared to go back to snorkeling. It didn't hold the same thrill it once did, because now I had been in the deep.

Far too many of us live complacently on the "surface" of life in our relationships with others and certainly in our relationship with God. We content ourselves "snorkeling around" with superficial relationships and with a shallow spirituality because we have not seen or tasted the pleasures of the deep. But once we do, we will never be happy to go back again.

Communication specialists for years have studied the steps toward true intimacy between people....friendships, marriages...and have found five clearly defined levels toward intimacy...going into "the deep waters" with others.

First, and most superficially, is "cliche" communication. This is the kind of interaction you may have on an elevator with someone you don't know at all, and who is going to be getting off at the next floor. You speak because it's awkward not to speak. "Nice day." "Terrible weather." "How are you today?" Most human interaction requires some level of cliche or "elevator" talk. But a relationship will never flourish there. There is no self-revelation at that level. This is sticking our toes in the conversational ocean, but not committing to it. It is tantamount to trying to speak of deep and abiding love with emojis.

The next level, going deeper, is what some refer to as "reporter talk." This is communication about others in our lives....family members, co-workers, friends or neighbors...and is basically the same kind of conversation you are having when you watch the news being reported. I can learn things from the news, but I will never get to know the newscaster based on what they are saying. Many relationships get stuck here, but again a flourishing relationship will never blossom at that level. We must go deeper.

Then, there is a "hinge point." At this level we risk an opinion, a judgement, or offer a suggestion or an idea to the person we're speaking with. If they agree with you, the question opens a doorway to a deeper and more meaningful level on the journey toward intimacy. If they disagree, we tend to travel up to a more superficial level of conversation...reporter talk or cliche because they're safer. We "come up for air."

If there is agreement with the one to whom you are speaking, you can move together into a conversation that truly begins to help you reveal yourself. Now we are at a "feeling" level of communication. To the women reading this, let me say quickly that if you are talking to a man he will most likely be uncomfortable here. Men tend to be very good at communicating ideas, opinions, and facts. But talking about how they feel is a different matter. When this is happening they will fidget, tap their pencil, look continuously at their phone or watch.

But if we don't get comfortable interacting on the "feeling" level we will never travel on to the deepest level of human and spiritual conversation and interaction: the level of intimacy...of bedrock, gut-level, open and honest communication. The last two levels have one important thing in common. At the "feeling" level and in "intimacy," there is self-revelation. We stop hiding behind our respective "bushes," and come out into the open...moving back toward that Garden experience that Adam and Eve knew of being "naked and not ashamed."

I need to add a caveat here. We will never know exactly the level of intimacy they knew, since they were the only human beings (besides the second Adam, Jesus Christ), who knew what it meant to be innocent. We are not, as Christians, innocent. We are forgiven, but sin still taints us and keeps us in hiding from God and others because of the shame that comes along with it.

But we can reach something of a deepening level of self-revelation with one another and before God. Psychologist Charles Lowery has suggested that intimacy can be simply defined as meaning "into-me-you-see." Something inside every person wants to experience that. Humanity was created by a God Who longs to self-reveal. We are wired to look for it. We want to know and be known by others at that level. We live in disappointment when it doesn't come.

Sadly in our modern culture we have substituted the hard work of intimacy for the fleeting pleasures of sex. Culture and the entertainment industry have convinced us that the sex act itself is the deepest possible level that one person can know with another, when in reality we can have a sexual relationship with people we barely even know. Some have sought to satisfy the longing each of us has for a true, intimate companionship and we trade it off for the "red stew" of satisfying our physical lust, as Esau the son of Isaac did.

We enter carelessly and casually into a sexual relationship that, while promising intimacy, is at the end a disappointing and shallow affair. It becomes sawdust in our mouths and proves toxic to our souls when in reality the God Who created sex said it is designed to happen between "one man...one woman. Period." Sex as an expression of a truly committed, God-created married couple's intimacy is the most wonderful thing that two people can know. Anything other than that is just snorkeling on the surface.

Going to the Deep Places with God

Now taking that brief outline, I would like to suggest that God invites us into an intimacy with Him as well. He keeps calling us out from our hiding places, out of our sin and shame, into the open air of communion and intimate knowledge of Him.

We begin that journey with PRAISE and THANKSGIVING. Praise and thanksgiving are the beckoning words used time after time for the worship of God's people coming to the temple. "Enter into His gates with thanksgiving...into His courts with praise."

The next deeper level is CONFESSION of our sin and AFFIRMATION of our forgiveness. To only confess our sins will lead us, not to freedom and intimacy with God, but into deeper shame and separation and ultimately despair. Judas took the sin of his betrayal and confessed it to a cohort of priests...and then hung himself. He never found the freedom of forgiveness. Peter took his public denial of Jesus...and equally heinous sin...but confessed it to the only One Who could assure his pardon. We must unveil our sins in the light of the cross or such confession will only lead to guilt, shame and death....not repentance.

Confession must be coupled with the affirmation that "Jesus paid it all." Our sin debt has been paid by the "spotless blood of a lamb." God does not want us sidetracked by obsessing over our faults. You have them. I have them. Let them go and see them already nailed to the cross of Jesus. He bled and died for your sins to be forgiven. All of them. Affirmation does that. Contrition alone...regrets and pain for our sin...

.will not get us on to the next level.

From there we move to INTERCESSION for others and PETI-TION for ourselves. Intercession, in a sense, is "reporter talk," but "reporter talk" can be an important and necessary part of most any meaningful conversation. God delights to hear our prayers offered on behalf of others. It is then that we may begin to pour out our own needs before Him...for ourselves specifically...in petition and supplication. "Let your requests be made known to God." What are you praying for today, specifically, that if God chooses to answer your prayer, you would *know* that He did? Praying "God bless all the missionaries" is a much different prayer than, "Lord, we pray that the VBS being planned in Haiti next week will draw at least 100 children who need to know the love of Jesus."

MEDITATION and CONTEMPLATION comes next. Much of our Bible study today is focused on learning some new truth, or traveling through some book or other organized study of Scripture. Most of our discipleship methods are built around that model. I'm going to go out on a limb that some may want to saw off here, but I find little in the Bible that speaks positively about learning new material. Now granted-there are places where we are told to "study to show ourselves approved unto God." Auditoriums are filled with Christians across the country interested in what new thing this or that teacher has to share. Yet many of their lives aren't changed by what they hear.

But I find so much more about how God desires that we go deeper in what we already know, and appropriate it as part of our life and let it become part of our blood and thought. It is through learning and practicing the art of meditation that we truly saturate and marinate in the truth of God's Word. Romans 12:1-2 tells us that we are to "be transformed by the renewing of our minds." This "renewing" involves an aspect of learning, but much in the way of spiritual strongholds and wrong thinking must be uprooted as well for the renewing to take place. The old must be rooted out and the new implanted. This will not happen only by study. It will happen as we learn to meditate on and assimilate the Word of God.

Too often we do Bible study like children going through a buffet line. They taste a little of this, and then reject it wanting to try something new. So they take some of that and chew it for a moment and then spit it out for the next dish. Always searching, but never arriving at the truth. Tasting, but never digesting. We seem to want to grow broad, and access more information and knowledge. God wants us to go deeper...and access Him.

When was the last time you took more than a few moments to think about something God said...a promise, a thought, a truth....and lingered to feel it's texture and taste the nuances of this spiritual meat? What if meditating on the Word of Life for a few extra minutes...lingering long enough for God to assimilate it into your spiritual makeup... became part of your daily walk with Him?

Then, as we pass through the preceding stages, we are invited to enter into the "Holiest of Holies" and come into the Presence of the Lord Himself. There we experience COMMUNION and ADORATION in the Presence of the One Who died to secure our salvation...Who purchased and redeemed us with such an awful and sacrificial price. We are now in the Presence of the One Who supremely loves us, completely "gets" us, has proven His eternal love by sacrifice, and Who beckons us with smiling face to draw near to Him with full assurance...to "come boldly before the throne of God...". In communion we draw near to God...to the One Who has made us one with Him through our Bridegroom, Jesus Christ. There we find the richest of fellowship and the deepest of intimacy possible under Heaven.

Of course our ultimate experience of communion and intimacy with God will come when we are "face to face" with Him in glory. There, we will "know as we are known." Nothing will be superficial. And nothing will be hidden. And there will be no tears, no sorrow, no crying... .and no shame....only adoration.

When was the last time you drew near to God like that? Did you know that this is His fervent desire for each of His children...to draw near to Him as a child to his father? In fact it is much more....it is the state that He longs for each of us to LIVE in...not just to visit on occasion. This is to be the normal state of the King's children...who have access to Him any time or in any situation.

I am confident of this one thing. Our experience in the hard place through this time has brought many, many of God's children to their knees in prayer, seeking the Father's face for mercy. For that fact I am grateful, and even though we did not receive the requests we had asked the fruit of fervent praying in that time has marked a lot of people. I have heard this testimony time after time.

So as we prayed, and sought God often with tears...and even as we prayed effectually and fervently through the hard place of Pam's cancer, we did not see the answer coming we and so many others had so passionately sought, we had to admit one thing: Never had we felt closer to God than we felt in this season of suffering and sorrow. In spite of not getting what we wanted from His hand, we instead were renewed in His Presence as we saw His face and felt His overwhelming peace. We knew an intimacy with God and each other.

And never did we love or trust our Father more.

PART TWO:

BETWEEN A HARD PLACE AND THE ROCK

Saturday. Saturday was a tough day for the disciples and the first followers of Jesus. The horror of Friday had ended. Death had taken their rabbi, their friend, their leader from them in the cruelest and most obvious way. The winding cloths and tomb held His body fast. But that was Saturday. And Sunday was coming....but it hadn't come yet.

We are people who live between the "now" of crucifixion and the "not yet" of resurrection. Saturday is not just a 24 hour stretch. It can feel like an eternity of waiting to see how God is going to turn our trials into testimonies. But until He does, we wait.

It's Saturday. But Sunday's coming.

CHAPTER 7:

BETWEEN THE MYSTERY AND CLARITY

"Movies are the prayers of the culture," so author Josh Larsen explains in his book by the same title. We hear what people yearn for at the deepest levels, how they imagine things are or should be, and even more how they think about God or religion or spirituality. One such "prayer" was offered a few years ago in a comedy entitled "Bruce Almighty," imagining a man named Bruce who suddenly found himself endowed with all the powers of the Almighty.

In an early piece of dialogue, Bruce has an interaction with his girlfriend, Grace, following a tough day before he was "empowered" from on high.

Grace: You know that everything happens for a reason.
Bruce: See, that I don't need. That is a cliché. That is not helpful to me. "A bird in the hand is worth two in the bush" . . . I have no bird, I have no bush. God has taken my bird and my bush.

Maybe that's just how you feel. You have no bird and no bush because God has taken them away. It's interesting that God usually gets blame for bad things with no corresponding credit for when things go well! But we can all sympathize with poor Bruce's plight. Bad things happen, and we think someone needs to take the blame. So we blame God.

I first encountered the writings and story of Rabbi Harold Kushner while I was a doctoral student at Southern Seminary in Louisville, Ky. His book, *When Bad Things Happen to Good People*, was just beginning to circulate and was on its way to being a New York Times best seller. We were assigned to read the book, and it was engaging and compelling. But wrong.

Kushner's story revealed his 8 year old son's diagnosis with a rare genetic disorder called "progeria." This disease horribly disfigures the victim, usually children, and ages them at an unusual rate. The pictures we saw of his son looked like a small, freakish, elderly man. His internal organs had also aged along with his skin. He walked with a little cane, suffered from arthritis and lost all of his hair. It is painful and at the time little was known about it.

His book chronicles their struggle with their little boy's illness and ultimate death from old age...at the age of 8. And then he begins, as a Jewish rabbi, to try and find meaning in their experience. He comes to raise this question for the reader: "If God is great (powerful) and God is good (merciful), why do bad things happen to people who don't deserve it?"

This is an age-old theological conundrum called a "theodicy." His conclusion shook the religious world at the time, and millions were reading his book. He decided that, if God was all-powerful (God is great) that means He could choose to do anything- including heal his son. And if God was good (meaning God is merciful) He would want to heal the boy. But both statements, Kushner concluded, could not be true and co-exist in the same person or even Deity.

So either God was NOT great, meaning there are certain things God would like to do, but doesn't have the power or that God is NOT good, meaning He is mean and malicious and cruel because He would not or was unwilling to do the good thing that was in His power to accomplish.

The controversy was in his conclusion. The rabbi decided it was easier for him to worship a God who was good but didn't always have the power to accomplish the good things He wanted rather than worship a God Who was powerful enough to do what he and his wife had prayed but chose, for whatever reason, not to do.

So this leaves us with a choice: Do we worship an all-powerful God with no compassion or a merciful, compassionate God who is limited in His power? His answer tells us a lot about the rabbi. Our view of God always does. AW Tozer has said, "What we think about when we think about God is the most important thing about us."

The problem with the rabbi's conclusion? The Jewish religion has no cross. There is no place for a crucified God. No place for unexplained and undeserved suffering as demonstrated at Calvary in the most incredible display of love and grace possible to consider. No place for the unlimited power of God and the deep love and mercy of God to meet mankind's sin.

Any understanding of human struggle and suffering that does not take this suffering God who became man into account will fall short in despair and questions that will drive us away from faith and will leave us only with questions....but no hope. Questions from the darkness. Mystery. The cross helps us see how God came down to enter into the suffering of humanity with us...not spare us from it. Without a cross we find ourselves impaled on the horns of Kushner's dilemma.

But the cross changes everything. One day as Pam was drawing near the end of her struggle with brain cancer, her breathing became extremely ragged and obviously her throat and lungs were filling with fluid. She sounded like she was drowning and no efforts to clear her airway or adjust her head would help. The congestion was part of her body dying. So I stood by helplessly as for excruciatingly long minutes her body struggled for breath.

As that day continued on I found myself, for the first time really, being angry. I forced myself to direct my question to God in the form of prayer. I told the Father that I truly believed He was a good, good Father....that He was sovereign and knew exactly where we were at every moment. And that I believed with all my heart that He knew exactly what Pam was experiencing and what I was feeling. Then I said, "God I don't understand. Why won't You stop this? Don't You get how horrible this is? Hasn't losing her ability to walk and use her hand and her ability to think and speak well been enough?"

And in that moment, the image of the cross flashed into my mind...the cross. Where the sinless Son of God hung for six bloody hours...the whole time gasping to breathe. The whole time struggling, as my wife was, with the effort to inhale...and then exhale life-giving oxygen. I knew and I taught that when a person died on the cross it was often due to suffocation, not blood loss. The Son of God died for our sins....struggling to breathe! He couldn't move either hand or foot. He could not speak without tremendous effort.

I stood silently contemplating that thought for several long moments. I realized that the Father not only knew what Pam was feeling but what I was feeling as I stood watching her. It was through the cross that God answered my questions in the darkness of those hours. It may or may not make a difference for Rabbi Kushner to understand that God completely knows what it means to watch a son suffer a horrible, unjust, and torturous death. But in that moment it made a huge difference to me. All the difference. He watched Jesus die the same way, and though He was more than powerful enough to take His only begotten Son down from the cross...away from the pain...away from the agony... .He chose not to do so.

We wrestle with our understanding and sense of human suffering and lose our way through the eyes of what we believe is "fair." "God," we say, "our circumstance, our situation, our suffering isn't fair and that means you should do something to stop it or You're not fair!" We allow our pain to blur how we think about the nature and character of God in such moments. Somewhere in us is still a form of idolatry that makes us believe God is there for our convenience to assure our happiness in life and that we always can get what we want.

I have wrestled through the "fairness" issue in our journey. "Father," I found myself thinking sometimes, "my wife has a brand new granddaughter that she wants to see grow up...we have a 40th wedding anniversary to commemorate with a celebration...Lord, she's just now ready to retire from her nursing career...." and on and on I could go. And I've found myself re-hearing the words I have spoken to so many: "Life is not fair." Bad things DO happen to really good people. And good things happen to really BAD people, which seems equally unfair. (Psalm 73:1-14)

Expecting fairness is a fairly recent development in the modern era. It is usually a "First World" question, meaning that the remainder of the world which is not as blessed as we are in developed countries don't have the leisure of pondering the question. Nor do they feel the entitlement to do so. I remembered being in middle school more than a few years ago....and I ended up getting caught up in a ring of trouble-makers in class who were always getting in trouble. This time they got the whole bunch of us in trouble and when the teacher (also the gym teacher and coach) came back into the room, he marched the whole bunch of guys (innocent me included) outside to the water fountain and paddled us HARD. He lifted the guys into the air as he paddled them. I watched in terror as one after the other, my comrades -in -trouble were lifted inches off the floor by the coach's glossy red fraternity paddle. And in that moment I pondered the unfairness of life for the first time as I gripped the edge of the fountain and waited for the paddle to connect with me.

We have all felt the sting of unfairness in life in one form or another. It's a part of the human condition. And we use our own plumbline, our own measuring stick, to determine what is or is not fair! Further, we expect God to comply with our assessment and instruments of measurement in this matter.

With this chapter, I have turned a corner into the most difficult subject that can be confronted for the believer in Jesus...or anyone else for that matter. The issue is, "Can God be both loving and good at the same time?" If God indeed is great and God is good, how can bad things happen to people who seemingly have done nothing to deserve such treatment? As I write these words, Hurricane Michael has already flooded several islands in the Caribbean and devastated portions of the western panhandle of Florida. I am a resident of the northern part of the state, and even our area, though not on the coast, could have been hit.

Surely in this storm people are suffering tragedy who are good people, who help others, who go to church and sincerely worship God. In the path of this monstrous hurricane are orphans that we have helped, fed and sheltered in Haiti. Though the island nation itself is anything but a wonderful, loving place to live (I've been in Haiti) there are innocent children affected as well as guilty adults who may steal or kill or practice voodoo.

And surely, by my limited human knowledge, if God has power, would He not want to intervene to stop it? Could He possibly have a purpose in allowing this that's better than saving the lives of those in the path of the storm who have nowhere to run or hide from its fury and it's rushing streams of uncontrollable water that wash away home and life?

A man who lived long ago asked much the same kind of questions about the mystery of God's will in the Old Testament book named for him. A righteous man, Job asked intense and passionate questions about this God Who seemed to relentlessly pursue him with death, disease, and discomfort.

But as Job learned, sometimes our questions are answered in silence...and sometimes they are answered out of the whirlwind. God is a mystery beyond human knowledge. There are things that God does...and doesn't do....and He is obliged to NO ONE to answer for His decisions. "Our God is in the heavens. He does whatever He pleases."

Now some may argue, "I can't follow a God I can't understand." Then I can assure you now that the God of the Bible will not be a God you can follow. He said, "My ways are not your ways, and my thoughts are not your thoughts. For as the heavens are higher than the earth, so are my ways higher than your ways." (Isaiah 55:8-9)

We do not serve a God Who can be understood....and subsequently controlled by us. As a clay pot cannot understand the thoughts of the potter at the wheel, so we cannot plumb the depths of God's ways or thoughts. He has revealed to us through His only begotten Son, the Lord Jesus Christ, everything we need to know of Him. (Hebrews 1:1-2). And that self-revelation was through One Whom the Bible called "a man of sorrows, and acquainted with grief" in the servant song of Isaiah 53.

Our God is not a god of Greek or Roman mythology who took pleasure in tormenting human beings, or who listened dispassionately to their cries. He is a God Who came and, in the incarnation through Jesus, felt our sorrow...wept our tears of pain, joy, and grief...and "was tempted in every way like us yet without sin."

He does not stand apart from the child crying in pain from hunger or fear in Haiti. He does not ignore the plea of the widow or orphan or refugee or flight of a sexually trafficked young woman. He knows your greatest pain and sorrow, fear and worry right now.

Even if you have lost your bird and your bush!

CHAPTER 8:

BETWEEN THE QUESTION
AND THE ANSWER

Give me the making of the songs of a nation,"
wrote Scottish thinker Andrew Fletcher,
"and I care not who makes its laws."

During my adolescence and young adult years I, like many of you, listened to a variety of music...much of which was not always well-enunciated by the singer. In other words, it was a mystery what the guy or lady was singing about. For some songs that was best because your parents wouldn't have let you listen if they really understood what the band was singing!

Still today, there are mysteries about some songs that were wildly popular, at least in the 60's and 70's when recording studios were just being built. And even if we could understand the words, we still couldn't get it!

Who knew what "In-a Gadda-Da-Vida, baby" meant? Or the lyrics to "A Whiter Shade of Pale?" Or the odd but catchy words of "Louie, Louie..." (once investigated by the FBI), other than "we gotta go now." While our love for Karaoke (which I have been told in Japanese might mean "can't sing") has helped clear up some of the mysteries, others still remain.

But then there were songs that were made popular that we could understand, but didn't realize how on target they really were until we had lived life for a while. One such song that sticks out to me was written by Justin Hayward and performed by his band, The Moody Blues. It's called "Questions:"

Why do we never get an answer
When we're knocking at the door
With a thousand million questions...

Why do we never get an answer
When we're knocking at the door
Because the truth is hard to swallow...
That's what the war of love is for.
        —*Justin Hayward, The Moody Blues*

Why do we never get an answer, when we're knocking at the door...? At least it seems that way sometimes, doesn't it? What a pointed question....especially when you are walking through a hard time. I've mentioned a few...but as Hayward and his band sang, there may be a "thousand million" questions that I didn't list in this chapter.

I went to pick up our granddaughter McCail early one morning because Pam was babysitting that day and I was the "transporter:" The Uber driver. I got paid with a smile from my granddaughter that warmed my day.

While I was picking her up, a text came from my brother informing me that he and my mother were at the ER in my hometown preparing to admit her. In one moment, there was joy and there was sorrow...mingled together. Paul reminds the church when we meet that we are to "rejoice with those who are happy and weep with those who sorrow."

With this section, I want to speak directly to the second group.

As a pastor, I hear three questions repeatedly from those who are walking through valleys and hardship in life. I'm generalizing, of course, and these tend to overlap, but they boil down to three:

Why do bad things happen? This question essentially is asking, "Is God there?" Is God there when I'm hurting? Is God fair? It seems sometimes that God is absent from our darkest days. Not always, and certainly He is not really absent, but it begs the question at times at least for some.

Does God care when I suffer? If God IS there, then the second question grows from the first. Does God care? Does He really even care that I'm drowning...that I'm weeping...that I'm lost and broken?

Is God aware? The third question that occurs in times of darkness is the question of loneliness. Is God with me? Am I facing this mountain alone, or is He truly One Who sticks "closer than a brother?"

Now again, I am simplifying since the purpose of this book is not to be a philosophy or apologetics textbook. These questions have hundreds of others burrowed deeply into them, and if I am evading a question important to you I will apologize now. But these themes recur in my counseling office as well as in hospital rooms, funeral homes, courtrooms and at scenes of accidents or even suicides.

Is God There?

This is the cry of every broken heart; every broken life on some level. "If God is really there, why is He allowing me to suffer evil, or abuse, or illness or death or divorce?" The question is this: Does the presence of moral evil or other forms of suffering disprove that there is a God?

When folks who are not believers ask this question, they ask it believing it firms up the argument that God does not really exist. For those who are believers, it is more a guttural cry of despair.

The secularist of our days believes that nothing in reality exists beyond what science can explain or technology can explore. Further, they believe also that science and technological advances have decisively disproved the need for faith or the existence of anything we cannot verify by scientific methodology. This is the prevailing philosophy of our day called "naturalism."

Richard Dawkins, one of the more popular atheistic writers of contemporary times, has stated that "Faith is like a mental illness..." and "it evades the need to think and evaluate the evidence." His position is echoed by many others, who do not believe that faith involves rational thought, and seeks instead to evade or discount scientific evidence.

In reality, there is no dichotomy between reason and faith, science and belief. Both have their role to play, and many philosophical and scientific thinkers have found faith to answer some of their most troubling questions and doubts. Unfortunately many who embrace scientific exploration at the same time embrace philosophical naturalism, which permits no room for an unseen, spiritual world and leads to an outright rejection of matters of faith.

But at the end of the day, philosophical inquiry and examination of scientific data will not alone lead one to faith. There is at some point a need for a step into an unseen dimension that we cannot examine under a microscope or make sense of in a philosophical textbook.

Certainly for a skeptic unexplained pain and suffering can drive one away from God if we let it. For others, the same pain and suffering can drive them toward embracing the God Who holds them even in the fire.

Several skeptical folks have unfolded stories they have experienced of unjust or horrific suffering they or someone they have loved have undergone. For these, the anger that flows from that experience and the need to "blame" someone or something for this forces them to believe against the existence of a good Creator...a loving God. In some of these instances it makes as much sense as a drunk driver who is caught blaming the police officer who stops him for being on duty.

Does the mystery of suffering lend itself to building faith or tearing it down? Truthfully it can do both. As some have cleverly stated, suffering can make us "bitter or better." I suppose that's true. Ironically, I write these words on the day commemorating the sixteenth anniversary of September 11. For Americans, and much of the world, this day marks a day of suffering and the overwhelming evil inherent in mankind willing to inflict it on others.

Thousands died in the collapsing buildings that tumbled into the streets of New York that infamous day. Our nation reeled in every way possible. Some shook their fists at a God Who would permit such unspeakable terror to take place. Others filled church buildings to pray to the same God for the survivors and for our country as we moved forward.

For some, the suffering of that day brought out the worst in them and a bloodlust for vengeance. For others, it brought courage and caring and love and resolve to be a part of the solution to our shared national wound. Some asked God for grace to continue. Others pointed to the lost lives and fallen structures as proof that no God could exist if something like that could take place. Others blamed God for not stopping it in the first place. God isn't good? God isn't fair?

It would have been tempting to "blame" God for what my wife experienced in her last months suffering from brain cancer. Or to "blame" God for not healing her, or not being fair...after all she already suffered through other types of cancer. She'd spent her life helping others deal with illness and recovery from surgery. "God, this cancer is Your fault! You could have stopped it!"

And yet it never occurred to us to do this. We both understood, as people of faith, that "the rain falls on the just and the unjust." Both of us knew of people with great faith who suffered enormously and paid a great price for that faith. Suffering is not an aberration of life, but a normal and expected dimension of it. The Bible does not counsel retreat from suffering, but faces the reality of disease, and pain, and evil head on.

The secular person may argue, "yes and you prayed to your imaginary 'God' and you see what it got you. Nothing!" So does unanswered prayer, or prayer answered differently than we prayed prove that God isn't there...doesn't hear...doesn't care?

My faith doesn't prevent me from hearing and considering those questions carefully but at the end, our faith still held fast...my faith still holds. These arguments did not...and cannot cut the foundation out from under those who place their feet upon the rock.

In spite of vehement denials to the contrary, every person has faith. A hospital staff was determined to function from a secular, non-faith based philosophy. Science ruled medicine, and there was no place made for faith. A Christian nurse, working on this staff, was in the room with a team of doctors who held this viewpoint. In a particular terminal patient's room a decision was made with the family to disconnect life support. The argument the doctor used with the patient's family was, "if we do this, at least we know his suffering will end." But the Christian nurse could not help but wonder, "and how do you know that?" Even in that statement lay a statement of faith that life ends all suffering. We all have faith...in something.

I believe that God was as present and active in the last days of Pam's earthly walk as He was the days and hours she spent offering praise in worship services or being the hands, feet, and eyes and mouth of Jesus as she cared for the hurting in hospitals.

Same God....different assignment. Is God there even when we suffer? My proof that He was still there is the fact that even though He did not do as we desire and restore Pam's physical "tent" is simply this:

I. Still. Believe. In spite of the worst, I still believe in a God Who hears us when we cry out. And though He may have not chosen to res- urrect Pam now, this does not mean He will not and has not already resurrected her to an eternal life that we can only imagine but now she gets to see face-to-face!

Does God Care?

Throughout the centuries of human history, the church has em- braced and embodied the message that God is a caring and compas- sionate Creator. Unlike the god of Deism, a view that became popular following the Enlightenment during the 1700's... a god who created a planet and then abandoned it and dispassionately observes as humanity unravels...the God clearly revealed in the pages of the Bible is a God Who weeps, Who cares, and Who has not abandoned even the least of His Creation. "I will never leave you nor forsake you," God reminds us in the Book of Hebrews. Not ever. Not for a moment.

God has branded this compassionate nature into His followers Who bear the name of Jesus. Since the beginning of the earliest days of the church, Christ followers have been the first to embrace a hurting and suffering world, and to be present in the pain of those around them. Christians do not run for the hills when others suffer. They run to the fire! Churches and believers have been the first to build hospitals, men- tal asylums for those suffering mental illness, and the first to inspire the creation of drugs and medications to help the hurting.

In the earliest days of the Christian movement, the followers of the Way taught by Jesus distinguished themselves by their willing- ness to go into plague afflicted areas and care for the ailing and bury the bodies of those who had died from the plague. These areas were quarantined by Rome in an efffort to contain the spread of the illness. But the believers in Jesus were the first to walk in, facing certain death as they did so, and care for those who suffered. It made an impact. It still does.

This incredible behavior bears witness to a compassionate God

Who wants His creation to know He is there...and that when suffering comes He is even more present. However the very existence of suffering is, to some, an evidence that a loving, caring God could not exist or else He would not allow suffering to be experienced.

Earlier in this book I wrote about the necessity of pain and the reality of suffering in our world. Again, our belief about suffering and evil is largely determined by our worldview—our assumptions about why the world and reality function as they do. The Christian worldview sees evil and suffering, not as part of God's original intention but an outworking of man's free will to choose to turn away from his Creator and go his own way.

Many books have been, and many more will be written to explain this philosophically and theologically. However for our purpose the concern is not why does suffering exist but what does God do in the face of it? Does He simply and apathetically turn away from it? Does He stay safely removed from it in heaven without staining Divine hands with our mess?

Or is our suffering and sin precisely the reason He sent a Savior...His only begotten Son...to feel our pain with us and to suffer not only with us but, ultimately, for us on the cross? He who came to bear our brokenness and bind up our wounds felt our sorrow, cried our tears and was heartbroken by the things that torment us.

He came, in fact, as a suffering servant to suffer as a sacrifice for our sin but also to leave us an example that we ourselves might know how to bear it. And not only this, He left on the earth His very Presence in the person of the Holy Spirit, the "Comforter" Who is able to comfort us in all our afflictions and suffering, loneliness and sorrow.

God is not absent from our suffering. He is most present as we experience it. He has, in Jesus, run to it. A man whose son was killed by an IED in Iraq came into his pastor's office one morning, placed his hands on the pastor's desk, leaned in and asked "Where was God when my son died?"

The pastor, stunned, quietly responded, "The same place He was when His Son died."

Is God Aware?

Have you ever wondered if your GPS "lady" hates you? I have. I always suspected she did, but now I've confirmed it. She's out to get me. No, I'm not being paranoid. Just stating the obvious.

On my pilgrimage following my wife's passing, I was traveling south of Knoxville, Tn to Georgia. I entered on the GPS the parameters of where I was going (actually, atop the highest mountain in Sky Valley, Georgia) to see a college friend who retired there.

The GPS routed me immediately off I-75 onto the back roads and into the back woods of North Carolina. And part of that route: Route 129 – Also known as "The Tail of the Dragon." Three-hundred eighteen turns in 11 miles. The curviest pavement in America. A place where bikers go to prove their mettle and impress their womenfolk and friends. A place where at least one person is killed each year and accidents are likely. A place where (as I learned at the completion and my entry into North Carolina) there is a monument called "The Tree of Shame," with hanging car and motorcycle parts for those who didn't successfully complete the drive.

I didn't know I was on the Tail of the Dragon. The GPS lady just forgot to mention that. She didn't offer a safer, alternate route. She should have said, "If you're feeling suicidal, here's the route for you." I only realized where I was when I came to the bottom.

When I arrived at the peak of the Tail, I turned a corner and two photographers were stationed there, standing in the middle of the road, to take what I had begun to realize were "the last pictures of this person ever seen alive" to help your next of kin identify you. I didn't buy one, (one of the companies had a tent called "Killboy") but I'm sure it would have shown a wide-eyed, white knuckled guy driving an SUV where only sports cars and motorcycles dare to tread.

But, as you might accurately conclude from this chapter, I did survive. And I learned something. Sometimes we find ourselves on "the dragon's tail" and we don't realize it...at least at first.

Life throws twists and turns our way that we never saw coming. A hurricane blows our way. A child gets arrested or expelled from school. A spouse leaves. Cancer takes a loved one. As I was finalizing this manuscript, Hurricane Michael came ashore on the Panhandle of Florida. Life went from a breezy Wednesday to total disruption and in some cases even death.

I drove the tail, mostly on four wheels, and tried to hang on and enjoy the scenery.

But I learned that's hard to do when a curved road on the edge of a mountain with NO guard rails is where you are at the moment. But that's life, isn't it?

Some of you are on "the Tail of the Dragon" today. Not by choice. You didn't see the curves coming. Fear meets you around every twist and turn. Uncertainty about your future looms. And the question begins to occur to us: "Does God even know where I am?"

A friend of mine whose five year old daughter was killed in a car accident a few years ago related the story of being in South America to dedicate an education center that was going to be named for his little girl. Friends had raised money to build it. People filled the building and camera crews were preparing to record his remarks.

When he arrived, the emotion of the moment and the experience of his grief flooded back in on him in crashing waves. He withdrew for a few moments to the solitude of an empty room and in the darkness, tried to compose himself. As he stood in silence the door slowly opened and a five year old, lovely Brazilian girl walked in. He had never seen her before. But she walked over to him as he leaned down to speak to her. Without a word, she put her arms around him, embraced him for several moments, and walked out.

Even in the middle of the expansive Amazon jungle, God sent

my friend a hug as though to say, "I know exactly where you are." Sometimes, that's all we need to know.

And it is enough. Yes, God is aware of our suffering. Yes, God is good.

Yes, God cares. No, God has not abandoned us even though it may feel He has. Call on the Lord. Trust Him in your distress. Wait patiently for Him to answer.

And be on the lookout for His Divine embrace as you do.

CHAPTER 9:

BETWEEN THE STRUGGLE
AND THE GLORY

Few who are believers find themselves in a time of difficulty, darkness, or pain without thinking about, reciting, or even posting on social media the familiar words of Romans 8:28 which affirm that "God is at work in every circumstance for our good." There is comfort in knowing that our seasons of suffering are not random circumstances or simply a matter of bad luck.

However, I doubt that a verse has been more incorrectly interpreted and misapplied than this one. Certainly, I believe that it is true to believe that God is "at work" in every circumstance. He is Sovereign. He knows the beginning from the end, and the duration from one to the other. And He knows the "why" of our circumstances.

This verse, however, is not an affirmation that everything that happens to us is "good," or is even the perfection of God's will for us. There are "ingredients" that go into the recipe of our lives that may be anything but the outworking of God's perfect will for us.

Anyone who has ever baked a cake understands this. The ingredients that go into a cake; flour, eggs, baking soda, butter, sugar...by themselves may or may not be palatable. In fact, they might even be bitter, or at least hard to swallow by themselves.

But when you mix them together and bake them to proper temperature, the whole is delicious even though it is made up of inedible ingredients when taken alone. Likewise, God's plan in our lives—the mystery of His will—has components that, at least at the time, may be hard to digest. We tend to want to judge too quickly the "cake" that God is baking.

I sat once at a horrific scene of tragic proportions in our community. A young mother who had recently been rendered handicapped by an automobile accident had, in despair and the depth of depression, taken the lives of her two young sons and then turned the gun on herself.

Her mother found the ghastly scene in her daughter's home and tried in vain to resuscitate her two young grandsons. As I sat with her after receiving a call from the sheriff's department, she wept uncontrollably as I noticed her legs were still splattered and her clothes stained with the blood of her grandchildren she had rushed to embrace.

The last thing I could have or would have said to her in that moment is "God is at work in this for your good." In that moment, I couldn't even bring myself to believe that as I looked on the horror of that scene and watched as the coroner's office wheeled three bodies from the house on stretchers.

As I have said to many going through their own experience of unexplained suffering, we tend to ask intellectual questions in such moments: "Why did this happen?" "Why is this happening to me?" The question "why" is a question that is premised on the belief that, if we could understand this, the pain would somehow be lessened.

In reality, our pain in that moment is not caused by confusion in our thinking, but the crushing of our hearts. We need our emotions fixed, not our thinking process. Having all the answers, even if we were capable of understanding them, would not fix our broken heart.

We need to know some things however. We need to know and believe that we are not alone when we are dropped into the abyss of our pain and sorrow. It is important for us to know and cling to that. And perhaps most of all, we need the comfort of knowing that God is present, even though in the moment He may not be taking action as we hoped and prayed.

It is in that moment that we need our faith to leap over the pain of the present for our trust to transcend and overwhelm our inability to proceed and process what is happening. Even though it may be incredibly hard to believe that God has not abandoned us to the random pain and evil that comes to us in life, it is essential that we reach beyond what we feel in the moment and believe some things about God.

In those moments when it feels as though the pain is overwhelming, we must accept that God has not lost control. To affirm our belief in a sovereign God, which the Bible clearly does, is to accept that He does not lose control, even in the ugliest of events that confront us. We must lose an immature and incorrect view of God that sees Him as a "cosmic genie" who exists to grant us our three wishes and spends His days in Heaven thinking of ways to make life easy for us.

To worship God as Sovereign means we accept the providence that comes, even when it is not good as easily as we accept providence that is good, as we would interpret it. Sometimes God's providence seems good, and sometimes anything but good to us.

I learned the lesson again recently when a property purchase for some land I had hoped our church could bid on fell through. The price was way beyond our pain threshold, so reluctantly I backed away from the deal. The next day in our staff meeting, we were sharing round-robin about ways we had seen God at work in the church during the past week. I drew a blank that morning, when suddenly the memory of the failed property deal came to the front of my mind. And I shared, "I saw God at work when He closed the door on the land we wanted." Nobody shouted hallelujah or praised the Lord. And yet, I reminded myself and everyone else that we should rejoice in that with as much energy as we would had the property worked out.

We don't celebrate in our disappointments. But if we believe that "all things work together for the good of those who love God and are called according to His purpose," then the closed door has as much spiritual significance as the open ones! This is true only if God is really Sovereign!

Can you rejoice in disappointment? A few years ago I was listening to a song that reminded me that there is only one letter difference between "disappointment..." and "His appointment." There is truly little difference, except in how we see it.

In the Old Testament book of Ruth, we learn that her mother-in-law Naomi lost a husband and both her sons. Her assessment after such loss and grief was that the Almighty had turned against her. "Do not call me Naomi," she counseled her Moabitess daughter in law. "Call me Mara." The name Mara meant "bitter."

Perhaps today it would seem to you that providence has turned bitter. That the Almighty God Who only seemed before to do good toward you or Whom you EXPECTED would only do good has suddenly turned against you. Life is now bitter. Disappointment seems to reign supreme.

The book of Job explores this mystery through a real life scenario of a man whom God regarded as "the most blameless man on earth." And yet God gave The Accuser (Satan) permission to begin to take family, possessions, and ultimately health away from Job to "test" him.

As the horrific news of family tragedy and death continued to pour in, Job's wife grew angry and disillusioned toward God. It was then that Job asked an important question we all must ponder: "Shall we receive good at the hand of God and not evil?" Is it right to think that the God Who has seemed unrelentingly good toward you through much of life has turned against you because your path has become difficult?

Such times of suffering bring us to a place of deep searching and even wondering if we know God at all? Especially this is so when it seems to you that you have faithfully and lovingly served Him and now you are being brought low through a hard time of testing and suffering.

You can trust God with the outcome. Helen Rosevere was a missionary nurse who devoted her life to serving the people of the Congo. Her life was anything but easy, but there came a day when an uprising in her village led to her capture and being held hostage.

For months, she was kept isolated. She was assaulted and mistreated during those long days. But the far worse torment came with the questions that were more persistent than the insects that were her constant companions. She wondered, "God why would You allow this to happen to me? Haven't I served You faithfully...selflessly...sacrificially? How can you allow the very people I have given my life to help to become my tormentors?"

One night in the darkness of her soul, God's answer came clearly to her. It came in the form of a question: "Helen, Can you trust me with this even if I never tell you why?" Her answer was "Father, YES."

Maybe God will never tell you "why" on this side of eternity. Can you live with unanswered questions; unhealed hurt; unsolved mysteries? If you really know and trust Your Father, you too can answer... "...YES."

PART 3:

BEYOND THE HARD PLACE TO THE HIGH PLACE

Psalm 91: "He who dwells in the shelter of the Most High will abide in the shadow of the Almighty..."

Can God take our hard questions? Where do you go with yours? God never rebuked Job when he threw question after question into the heavens in response to his unexplained "hard place." God is our Rock, and He is our salvation, our stronghold, and our deliverer. There is none like Him. He is Sovereign. He is eternally stable...and He is able to hear us in our weakness, our complaining, and our doubts. And at the end of it all, we find ourselves throwing ourselves upon His stability, His unchangeable and unwavering character, and His faithfulness. He is our Rock.

There is none other.

CHAPTER 10:

ENCOUNTERING HOPE IN THE HARD PLACES

We live a story each day that is not complete. It is unfinished. Those who would convince themselves that life is simply lived and then over when death comes are people who have the most difficulty in the hard places. As Paul said of those in 1 Corinthians 15 who have no faith in the resurrection, we would be "of all men most to be pitied if the dead are not raised." But if we know the hard place is not the end of the story, we can endure. And we have hope that points us beyond our present reality into a life that is eternal.

As I write these words, I learned just a few hours before of a young couple who lost a baby several months in the womb. The child had been prayed for, wanted, and had come about after tremendous and even expensive effort. But he came too soon, and left his parents before they heard his first cry.

I know the couple. They love God...deeply. But their hope is resilient, and they will endure.

As I complete this manuscript, I am processing the pictures and stories of a horrific collision of cars and vans and trucks on 1-75 south near Gainesville, Florida. Fifty gallons of diesel fuel spilled on the pavement fueling the flames of the fire. In the flames, at least five children died who were on their way to Disney World, traveling in their church van from Louisiana. The youngest in the vehicle was eight years old.

How do we find hope in scenes like these?

In his book *Suffering*, Paul David Tripp wrote:

In a moment your life can change dramatically. In a moment the future that seemed so sure evaporates before your eyes. In a moment that loved one whom you thought would walk with you for the rest of your days walks away or is taken away, never to return again. In a single conversation you are told that sickness will rob you of your physical vitality. In a moment an injury changes your life forever. Yes, life changes in little ordinary moments or in dramatic big moments. You and I have no power to make our lives stay as they are. We have no power to welcome only the good things into our lives and ward off the bad things. We cannot assure ourselves that we will always be loved, protected, and healthy or will always have the resources we need. We cannot put security systems in our lives to protect us from fear and sorrow. When we're going through dark and tough things, we cannot guarantee ourselves that these will pass and that things will get better. We're all dealing with forces bigger and more powerful than we are. It only takes the wicked whip of a tornado or the fearsome power of a hurricane to remind us of how small we are, how fragile our lives are, and how little power we actually have.

In a matter of a very few hours, hurricane force winds blew away normalcy for tens of thousands and for some even life itself in the Florida panhandle after Hurricane Michael's onslaught in the autumn of 2018. But on signs on church and business locations, and painted in graffiti on the side of buildings, you can read the echoes of hope in the disaster: "We will rebuild!"

Hope can look squarely in the eye at the worst of circumstances, and even beyond reason or rational thought scream back, "I will not let this defeat me!" For some this is just wishful thinking.

But for the ones who have built their house on the solid rock of trust in Jesus Christ and in His Word, hope is a given. It comes with the territory. It can be anticipated, and even expected that hope will accompany you beyond the tragedies, the misfortunes, and the disasters that we find ourselves confronting.

The believer in Jesus Christ possesses a "living hope:"

*In God's great grace He has given us new birth into a **living hope** through the resurrection of Jesus Christ from the dead, and into an inheritance that can never perish, or spoil, or fade. This inheritance is kept forever for you."* (1 Peter 1:3-4)

In Hebrews 6:19 we read, *"We have **this hope** as an anchor for the soul, firm and secure."* It may surprise you to learn that the earliest Christian symbol was not a cross, nor was it the "ichthus" fish.

It was an anchor. This anchor represented hope that keeps us "firm and secure." But an anchor alone is an albatross that ultimately will do nothing but cause you to sink faster. The anchor is only as good as the strength of the object to which it is secured.

Only the solid Rock Who is Jesus, can bring that security. He is the only One with the real power to do this. In the words of the old hymn, only He can "anchor my soul in the haven of rest."

"My strength," God told the Apostle Paul during a time of great difficulty, "is made perfect in your weakness." (2 Corinthians 12:7-10). Maybe more than anything else, this explains why we as Christians find ourselves in "tight spots" and the hard places. As we look inside and outside ourselves and find no one else to count on, God has the opportunity to demonstrate His perfect strength in our imperfect weakness.

We are really unsure of what the Apostle Paul was referring to as his "thorn in the flesh."

The word "thorn" is misleading in English. The Greek uses the word "stakos," more a tent peg than a sharp point on a rose bush. It was used sometimes as an instrument of torture in those days. But there is no evidence of what his persistent struggle may have been.

Some faithful missionary friends I know have served in some of the hardest places on the planet. In one of their first assignments, they lived in an area rife with malaria, and their whole family eventually contracted it. There are reports of those who get malaria that it feels at times like a stake is being driven through your temple. And while the symptoms can be managed with medication, it is a condition that can continue to recur.

There is some good evidence, based on where Paul was traveling and the austere conditions in which he traveled, that malaria was his thorn. In one place in the New Testament he referred to an eye problem that was blinding him. It could have been he was losing his eyesight due to an illness or an injury sustained. Maybe hours of reading and writing in darkened prison cells were taking their toll. The best we can do is speculate. What we don't have to wonder about is how Paul perceived his condition. He saw it as "a messenger of Satan sent to torment me."

But in his torment there was another possibility he saw, and that was God allowed this difficulty to humble him. "Because of the visions...." God was "balancing out" what Paul was experiencing spiritually, but grounding him with earthly struggles that reminded him of his humanity. They kept his feet on the ground, so to speak.

We need similar reminders, as Christ-followers, that our pathway will be marked with moments of spiritual exhilaration, as well as with humiliation. God's grace carries us into...and through both places. Sometimes, as the cross teaches us, they happen simultaneously.

As I drove through the wreckage left by Hurricane Michael in Florida, I passed nightclubs and liquor stores that had been demolished...as well as houses of worship. "The rain falls on the just and the unjust," and so, obviously, do hurricanes. God's common grace...and sometimes difficulty... touches all who are part of this sin-saturated world.

In one instance the extremity of the situation is an opportunity for God to shout and get the attention of a deaf and dying world. In the other, the same circumstance is an opportunity for God to show Himself strong in our weakness and brokenness.

For those whose hope is in Christ, we can say with Paul that God's grace is sufficient for us. "For when we are weak, then we are strong." It is an irony, a contradiction of terms almost, until you have experienced exactly what this means. When our weakness threatens to overwhelm us, it is then that God's grace rushes in and lifts us up...and holds us through the storm that threatens to destroy us. God is not looking for strong people, but for ones who are willing to be broken...even shattered...by His grace. Maybe we could say "what makes us weaker makes us stronger!"

Lee Stroebel tells of a man named Jeff Miller who was on a fateful flight from Denver to Chicago O'Hare International Airport. While airborne, the plane suddenly lurched and shuttered violently. An engine had exploded and the steering was badly damaged.

He described the next moments as it became obvious the plane was going to attempt an emergency landing in Sioux City, Iowa. People in seats around him trembled in fear and some wept. A few swallowed another drink and assured themselves that it was all going to be fine.

But Jeff prayed. He prayed for the people around him, and he prayed for himself. "Lord," he prayed, "I want to live, but I know if I don't I'll be with you and you'll take care of my family."

He braced for a violent death that never came. The plane scraped onto the runway, cartwheeled, and broke apart, exploding into orange flames. Jeff's portion of the fuselage broke away from the rest of the plane, landed in a cornfield and came to a stop upside down. Jeff hung suspended in his seat, without a scratch on him.

In his testimony he recounted what it was like to be in that kind of situation. He said, "It was scary but at the same time I was full of hope. There was hope if I lived, and there was the hope that if I died, I would be with Christ. It says in Psalm 118:6, *"What can anybody do to you if your hope is in the Lord?"*

The airplane Jeff was on had both Christians and non-Christians aboard. The same circumstance did different things to each person. For the believer, God again showed Himself perfect in strength through their weakness. For some of those without Christ it became the last chance they would ever receive to call out to Him for salvation.

Hope for many is an elusive and misunderstood commodity. It becomes for some simply positive thinking; a topic for a motivational speech. I heard a person say recently that the things that people say at funerals are just wishes. For some I'm sure that's true. Death becomes a time of "whistling in the dark." But hope that is rooted and grounded in Jesus Christ is hope that will sustain us when we need it.

Atheism as a system of thought is devoid of hope. Those who advocate for a non-existent God Who made us, shapes us, and controls our destiny have very thin lines to hang their hopes on. Bertram Russell, one of the most prolific and well-known spokesmen for atheism, wrote this about mankind:

His origins, his growth, his hopes and fears, his loves and his beliefs, are but the outcome of accidental collocations of atoms...The whole example of man's achievement must inevitably be buried beneath the debris of a universe in ruins.

How different than the proclamation of hope found in the Gospel of Jesus Christ!

Not only that, but we rejoice in our sufferings, knowing that suffering produces endurance, and endurance produces character, and character produces hope, and hope does not put us to shame, because God's love has been poured into our hearts through the Holy Spirit who has been given to us. (Romans 5:3-5 ESV)

We have a hope, the origin of which is grounded in the love of God for us...not an accidental "collocation of atoms," but a real hope that fits us to live well in a real world. It is purposeful, powerful, and available to all who will ask for it.

We do not have to live in a world devoid of hope. We do not have to endure difficulty, and hard places, or even face the end of our lives without hope. "*Hope does not put us to shame,*" the Bible says. It will not let us down in the hard place.

In fact, it is the only way to get beyond them.

CHAPTER 11:

EMBRACING LIFE BEYOND THE GRAVE

It's no secret. People fear dying. They fear the experience of leaving their bodies, of being separated from their families, of pain that may accompany their last days, and of the deterioration of their physical bodies.

It's no secret. Fully one-third of Americans have confessed to being unable to think about, talk about, or face the thought of their own death. They go to great lengths to cover their fears: substance abuse is an option for some; others cover their fear by consuming their lives with work or career, money and travel, or absorption with pornography, sex, or other entertainment. Still others collapse into fear-based psychological symptoms because they don't know how to cope with what they don't know.

These mechanisms are a means of attempting to blot out the unpleasant statistic that one out of one die. There is no promise that the normal life expectancy in America will be ours. People die young-frequently. For some death is self-inflicted, as they find the uncertainty of life unendurable. According to the most recent CDC records, suicide is the third leading cause of death among 18-24 year olds in America. I was visited in my office as I was working on this chapter by the police chaplain of the local sheriff's office of our Florida county. He was telling me about a young deputy who had just died of a self-inflicted gunshot wound, leaving a bewildered wife and family behind.

"It is appointed to man once to die, and after this the judgment." (Hebrews 9:27)

Others cope by creating fanciful options as to what will face us when death comes. We all will go to Heaven...with our pets, some believe. Others believe that karma will assure we will return in a suitable life form in an endless cycle of reincarnation, kind of a spiritual do-over, in spite of the clear statement in the Bible that death comes to us only once...not in an endless series of deaths and rebirths.

Still others tell themselves that death is a deep, dreamless sleep-state, and yet many places in the Bible affirm the reality of a continuation of life after death, some in the arms of God in Heaven and others as the focus of His eternal wrath. We create a fantasy that suits our temperament, and just live assuming that's how it will be. But ultimately the reality makes us come face-to-face with death.

In the Middle Ages, the Black Plague inspired a children's song that sometimes kids will sing today:

A ring around the rosies, a pocket full of posies;
Ashes, ashes we all fall down.

Maybe you sang it, or taught it to your children without fully pondering the words. It was a way to help children confront the reality of death. Its a "whistling through the graveyard" kind of tune. Posies were stuffed into people's pockets because they made them sneeze, and it was believed that sneezing eliminated the plague from your system. "We all fall down," the refrain tells us. We all fall down...in death.

"If a man dies, will he live again?" Job asked in Job 14:14. It continues to be the most important and pressing question any person can ask. And it was finally answered by Jesus Christ, the One Who proclaimed "I am the resurrection and the life. He who believes in me will

live, even though they die." (John 11:25)

On Easter Sunday, on the third day, Jesus rose again after His own public, shameful, but sacrificial death on the cross. He arose victoriously from a grave that could not keep Him and over death that could not hold Him. Today if you visit the tomb of Confucius, the great Chinese philosopher, his body is still there. Visit the tomb of Mohammed, the prophet of Islam, and his body is still there. Visit the tomb of Joseph Smith, the founder of Mormonism, and his body is still there. You can even visit the tomb of Mary Baker Eddy, founder of the Christian Science movement...and her body is there.

You can visit the tomb of Jesus Christ, but *His body isn't there!* Only Jesus overcame the grave and defeated it's power. Only Jesus came back from death.

But it wasn't just His victory over death that was celebrated on Easter Sunday morning but our victory as well if we believe He arose. And because He rose from the dead, certain benefits are promised those Who have put their faith and trust and confidence in Him.

There is No Fear of Death

Through Jesus' victorious resurrection, the fear of death was overcome. Hebrews 2:12 says that Jesus freed those who "all their lives were held captive to the fear of death." This fear is a familiar face to many. Death is so mysterious, so terrifying to us. We seek all our lives to either deny it or to numb the fear. But through Christ, the chains of fear were broken. Death is not a hopeless end, but in Jesus Christ an endless hope to those who believe. It holds the prospect of homecoming for the believer...of stepping into the arms of a familiar Friend Who has purchased our way home with His blood.

There is No End of Life

Did you know it is Biblically incorrect to speak of death in connection to Christians? Now of course, there is the spiritual reality and necessity of "dying daily" to ourselves. But when our bodies cease to function, our lives do not end. Not for a moment. "Absent from the body, present with the Lord" (2 Corinthians 5:6-8) will be our experience. Jesus died on the cross, experiencing everything that death meant, so we wouldn't have to!

A man was driving in the countryside with his young son when a large black bumblebee flew through an open window. The boy immediately flew into a panic because he was severely allergic to bee stings. Seeing his son's panic, the father reached out and grabbed the bee in his fist, allowing it to sting him, then opened his hand and let the powerless insect fly out. The boy again began to panic, but the father calmed and reassured him by saying over and over, "the bee can't sting you...it stung me!" And he showed his son the swollen red spot where the stinger of the bee entered his hand...and stayed.

Like a bee without a sting, death can buzz around us and generate fear if we let it. But the "sting" of death, the penalty of the law, has already stung Jesus for us. "Where O death is your sting? Where, O grave is your victory?" asked Paul in 1 Corinthians. It has no power to sting those whose trust is in Jesus. He bore the sting of death, the full penalty of sin, for us!

Christians do not die. Instead they "sleep" when their bodies cease to have life in them. But it is only our bodies that sleep...not our eternal spirit. When we are born again, we receive eternal life. That is life that begins in that moment and does not ever end...even when our bodies rest in death. And though the body of the believer "sleeps," which is the obvious thing we see with our eyes, the invisible and eternal spirit of that individual awakens in the presence of the Father...more alive than ever before. (2 Corinthians 5:7)

In fact, the very word "cemetery" is taken from a Greek word that means "sleeping place." The early Christians named their graveyards "cemeteries" to acknowledge this reality. A Christian never dies. Ever. Death was once for all defeated in Christ, and He died so that those who follow Him would never have to experience it.

This reality is emphasized in 1 Thessalonians 4 where Paul refers to those who have gone on before us as "sleeping."

Brothers I do not want you to be uninformed about those who sleep in death, so that you will not grieve like those who have no hope. (1 Thessalonians 4:13)

In fact every time death is talked about in reference to a believer it is referred to as sleep in the New Testament. It is never called "death" in relationship to the believer. In Christ, there is no end of life...only a transition to an eternal state and there to wait for the eventual day that their resting bodies will be awakened and reunited with their spirits. One day, the "sleeping places" will give up those bodies, as will every other place the body has gone.

"No guilt in life, no fear in death, this is the power of Christ in me."

—In Christ Alone

There is a Promise Waiting

Our security rests on a promise Christ made to us. He said, *"Let not your hearts be troubled. You believe in God, believe also in Me. In My Father's house are many dwelling places. If it were not so I would have told you. I go to prepare a place for you, and if I go and prepare a place for you, I will come again and receive you to Myself, that where I am there you may also be."* (John 14:1-3)

We sometimes "undersell" the value of having a heavenly home waiting. We seldom dwell on it or give it a second thought. C.S. Lewis framed our problem well. He wrote,

We are half-hearted creatures, fooling about with drink and sex and ambition when infinite joy is offered us, like an ignorant child

105

who wants to go on making mud pies in a slum because he cannot imagine what is meant by the offer of a holiday at the sea.

I will have to candidly admit that, until my wife's diagnosis with a terminal illness, we left much of our thoughts about Heaven in the theoretical category too. Life for us was full, and busy, and happy. We had everything we needed, and much of what we wanted including a wonderful new granddaughter. Life was fulfilling for us on earth.

Heaven? Well, we really don't have much time to think about that. Then, the phrase "terminal cancer" was attached to my bride. Suddenly, ALL we wanted to think about, study about, and hear about was Heaven. Pam loved for me to read the passages in the Bible to her that talk about Heaven, and I drank them in myself like a man dying of thirst.

I needed to know...to increase my faith...that Heaven was real. That the promises Jesus made us were sure. The confidence we received from knowing those things literally carried us through the last weeks and months of her life. And they still carry me, though for her faith is over. She no longer sees "through a glass darkly." She now sees face-to-face!

A Heavenly hope will carry you through the hard times, through times in the pit, through times of confusion, heartache, brokenness, and even death. It will carry you beyond the difficulties of life.

It did this for Paul. This man who, by his own description, was beaten with rods and whips on five occasions, shipwrecked at sea three times, nearly stoned to death, was left without water, food, and clothing...declared his Heavenly hope in Romans 8:16:

I consider that our present sufferings are not worth comparing with the glory that will be revealed in us.

And later he wrote,

Eye has not seen, ear has not heard, nor has it entered the heart of man the things that God has prepared for those who love Him.

CS Lewis offers help once again. He wrote,

If I find in myself a desire which no experience on earth can satisfy, the most probable explanation is that I was made for another world.

This world was never intended to fully satisfy our longings for the eternal. It can only faintly point the way to the only One Who will truly meet our deepest needs. No person on earth, no relationship on earth, no experience on earth, and no possession on earth can ultimately grant this fulfillment.

Only Heaven does that. And because of Christ, all that Heaven holds is ours! We have "an inheritance laid up for us in heaven." (1 Peter 1:4). And we will be restless on this planet and in this physical body until we see our Savior face to face.

In that moment, we will truly know the fullness of life beyond. Until then we wait in confidence that all of these promises...every last one...will be kept!

And Lord, haste the day when our faith shall be sight
The clouds be rolled back like a scroll
The trump shall resound, and the Lord shall descend
Even so, it is well with my soul.
—It is Well with My Soul, Horatio Spafford

CHAPTER 12:

FINDING OUR FOREVER PLACE

The universal desire to have a home has preoccupied humanity for all of our existence. From the earliest days of those whose lives were characterized by wandering as nomads and living in tents, to the days of early conquest of lands previously undiscovered, people have sought for...indeed longed for a home that would be theirs forever.

Since the Garden of Eden, mankind has been homeless...rootless...wandering. One of the earliest confessions of faith in the Old Testament said, "My father was a wandering Aramean." (Deuteronomy 26:5). The people of Israel understood and felt their rootlessness...and they longed for a city "whose builder and maker was God."

Somehow we intuitively know that our present "home," our present circumstance, whether a shack on the side of a hill or a glorious mansion, is not going to last forever. It will one day deteriorate, or be passed on to the next generation. We are all, in that sense, truly "homeless."

I have visited two historic mansions in my lifetime. One I stayed in, and the other I paid admission to walk through. The first was a mansion built by the Vanderbilt family now known as Biltmore Estate. Hundreds of thousands of people have walked the halls of this extravagant and beautifully appointed 250-room mansion.

The second was a vacation retreat built by the Carnegie family. The Greyfield Inn sits on Cumberland Island in Georgia and has been the vacation spot of choice for the Kennedy family. It was the romantic spot chosen by John Kennedy when he married Caroline before their fatal plane crash.

I have walked the halls, looked in closets and secret chambers, and even walked through the Olympic-size swimming pool in the basement of the Biltmore estate. We saw things we had never seen before and you leave wondering how they even manage to live in such an expansive house.

But one thing I can assure you I did not see. I did not see the people who built these opulent homes walking the halls. Their pictures were there; portraits painted in the early years of the Twenty First century. But they were gone.

A young man leaned over to the accountant of a wealthy man as they stood together at the deceased millionaire's gravesite. He asked his mentor, "How much did he leave behind?"
The older man replied, "Every bit of it."

Some of the earliest of pioneer hymns sung as Americans moved westward expressed this reality; "I've got a mansion just over the hilltop..." or "I've got a home in gloryland that outshines the sun." While their eyes might have been temporarily fixed on the prospect of a home more permanent than the covered wagons they traveled in, they still knew deep in their hearts that any home built on the dirt of this world was going to be temporary.

We all know that, I think. For some, this thought creates anxiety. For others, whose understanding is more spiritually rooted, it brings hope. Nothing this world can offer will fully satisfy the deepest longings in us. We are spiritual beings, and as such long for a spiritual home.

The Homeless Savior

No one understands homelessness like Jesus. In His birth, He was laid as an infant in a borrowed manger. In His life, He said, "Foxes of the earth have holes, and birds of the air have nests, but the Son of Man has nowhere to lay His head." (Matthew 10:24) And even in His death, His crucified and crushed body was wrapped in cloths and laid in a borrowed tomb. No deed of land ever bore His name. No address was attached to Jesus of Nazareth on earth.

But the same would be true of His followers, though to a lesser extent. Jesus was not against people owning property, nor does the Bible condemn such. However, property and homes and finances must ever be held lightly.

Methodist pastor John Wesley was visiting a wealthy landowner who had invited him for dinner. After a meal suitable for a king, the landowner took Wesley on a horse ride to survey his property. When the tour of the man's land holdings was completed, he looked at the circuit riding preacher and said, "Well, Mr Wesley, what do you think?" Wesley, quiet in contemplation, looked at the man and replied, "I think it's going to be very hard for you to leave all of this behind."

The perspective of the Bible is that all we own is temporary, and one day we will leave land and riches and property and stocks and any physical thing behind. "This world is not my home, I'm just a-passin' through; my home awaits in glory land somewhere beyond the blue." Don't get attached to the things God allows you to manage and use. They're a temporary holding.

Several have repeated the story of life being like the game of Monopoly. During the hours it takes to play the game, a player can become a wealthy land and property owner, a railroad tycoon, and zip around the board in a sports car. But when the game is over, all of the property, all of the railroad stocks, all of the houses and hotels, all the money, and even the game pieces go back in the box. And one day, you too will go back in the box.

Those who follow the Lamb of God must accept this viewpoint. Those who walked with Jesus followed him into a life of itinerant, rootless ministry. The homes they stayed in were homes belonging to friends; not their own. The hospitality received was a result of the kindness of those assorted friends and strangers.

A Promise to the Homeless

A few hours before His arrest in the Garden of Gethsemane Jesus sat with His disciples as they shared Passover supper. This became the first time the Lord's Supper would be shared as well. But in their time around this intimate table, Jesus began the process of preparing His disciples for the shock of His passion that would begin in mere hours from then.

He began by stabilizing them internally. "Don't let your hearts be troubled; you believe in God, believe also in Me..." These words have brought comfort and hope to millions since the evening they were first spoken by Jesus. In essence, He challenged them not to allow the impending events to shake their faith or to agitate their hearts.

They have brought comfort and stability to those walking in their own times of struggle and trial and crucifixion for over two millennia. They have been read over the open caskets of a deceased loved one, at a graveside, in hospital rooms and Hospice wards, and even on the deck of an aircraft carrier to soldiers preparing to go into battle.

They speak of a comfort that comes when our faith is securely placed in the only One Who can bring peace and stability into our hearts. "You believe in God..." This affirmation is certainly a needed one. But Jesus was saying in essence that simply believing in God is not enough... "believe also in Me." The God-man Who came to reveal the Father to us is the only One Who can finally and truly convey this stability and comfort to us in the midst of our turmoil.

The Promise of A Lasting Home

It was then that Jesus shared a promise they could all embrace. It was the promise of a home, not on the earth, but in heavenly dwellings. "I am going to prepare a place for you." This promise was, on the first level, a promise made by the bridegroom to the bride. It was a promise that would have been heard akin to a marriage invitation.

In the Middle Eastern world of that day, most marriages had already been arranged by the fathers. Sometimes these marriages were made to join land holdings, or to assure a peaceful relationship between neighbors. But there was no random marriage proposals made in that day. It was too important a thing to be left to the whims of the heart.

The marriage of Christ and His bride, the Church, is in essence the truest "arranged marriage." We have been promised to Jesus from "before the foundations of the earth." And now, He is acting as a responsible bridegroom toward His bride. He's going to "make a place;" to "prepare a place," a home, for His bride.

We misread this text sometimes. The promise Jesus was making was "I am going to (do the work necessary) to make a place for You in my Father's house." He taught them and us that His Father's house has many rooms, and more than enough space for all Who would join in this marriage. But He did not go back to Heaven to pick up a carpenter's hammer. The work necessary to prepare a place for them was accomplished when He laid down on a rough, wooden cross and was Himself nailed there to die.

The bridegroom of this day would go away to his father's property and there perhaps add a room for him and his new bride to live in. A few years ago while on a trip in Macedonia, we stayed with a missionary family who had done just that. In that country since property is very expensive, it was customary for children to build a level onto their father's house and create a small apartment or second house for them and their children to live. Some homes would be three or four stories depending on the size of the family.

In Biblical times, the problem would be knowing the exact time of the arrival of the groom after he had complete the house. Without modern means of communication, his arrival could be roughly estimated but not pinpointed. Therefore, everyone must remain ready for his return.

This makes some of the parables make more sense; the bridesmaids waiting with oil in their lamps for instance. What were they waiting for? The coming of the groom! They would light his path and lead him to the location of the wedding. They dared not allow their oil to run out.

It is not difficult for us to connect the dots between this common social event and the second coming of Jesus. Like the bridesmaids, we must remain vigilant and watchful and ready. Like the bride, we do not know "the day or the hour" of His return...only that He promised He would. "If I go and prepare a place for you, I will come again and receive you to Myself that where I am there you may also be."

Jesus promised them...and us...a home that will not ever require us to leave. It will be a home built on His promises, His sacrifice, and His blood. And it has been prepared for you!

A More Permanent Home

We attach a lot of meaning to our earthly dwellings. They get embedded with memory and emotion and experience and the stuff that makes life...well...life!

I well remember the home our family lived in from the time of my fourteenth birthday. I experienced middle school, high school, early college and the first days of dating Pam. I played ping pong and pool in the basement with friends, clanged through my first garage bands, changed from an adolescent to a young man, cut myself shaving for the first time, and cut grass for the first (but not the last!) time.

Memories of Thanksgiving and Christmas, birthdays, first crushes, and winter snowfall abound in my mind. So do memories of my father's last two years battling a brain tumor, and my mother's last years of living there after his passing.

The house was as thick with memories as Mom's old iron skillet, handed down to her from her mother, was thick with grease from hundreds of meals of fried potatoes and cornbread cooked over the years.

Like those meals once enjoyed, the memories still coated the walls and rooms and care were imbedded in the walls and floors and carpeting of the house.

And it was not easy for me and my brother to release it after Mom's death. We weren't selling brick and drywall and carpet. We were selling something of ourselves.

The same can be said, of course, of the memories that still haunt me of mine and Pam's first house; one with axles. We bought a mobile home for our first year or so together, before moving on to college and rented apartments and house-sitting for professors.

The memories still live in my mind of those places- their look and feel and fragrance. But even as I sit in the home Pam and I lived in almost 13 years together...I realize one thing. It isn't permanent. Nothing we have is.

We leave in temporary dwellings. Moses talked to the people of Israel about moving into homes they had not built as they overtook the Promised Land. But though it was the land of promise, it was not a place of permanent dwellings. Just as someone lived in the house they occupied before them , someone will likely live there after them. We. Own. Nothing.

"That which is seen is temporary..." the Apostle Paul reminds us. Everything we can see and experience with our eyes or our other senses will pass away. Everything. "That which is unseen is eternal." (2 Corinthians 4:16)

Groaning Bodies and Sagging Tents

We live not only in temporary homes on earth: we also live in temporary bodies. Paul reminded us, again, that we live essentially in tents. "We know that these tents we live in will pass away." One day, our tent will collapse. This the Bible calls death.

Nobody wants to live in a tent. I've been in several urban areas where homelessness is common, and have walked through the makeshift neighborhoods set up between buildings or under bridges. The "tents" the homeless construct are often old cardboard boxes, or articles of clothing strung together for a temporary roof. It is now their home.

But nobody aspires to live long in such a place, whether a homeless encampment or even camping recreationally. My parents used to take us camping in nearby state parks in Kentucky. We would go, sometimes for a long weekend, and sometimes for a longer stay. And we would sleep...in tents.

I made some profound life decisions during those times. First, I never took my family camping! It just never appealed to me. But second, I decided that I did not aspire to live my life in a tent...a canvas that leaked water in the rain...held together with sagging tent poles and non-functioning zipper!

And yet, all of us live in a tent...with varying degrees of wrinkling and leaking and sagging...that is one day going to collapse. Then, it is important to know we have a "home awaitin' in gloryland just beyond the blue." Our temporary home will be gone. Our "place" will be a place of eternal separation from God forever and "prepared for the devil and his angels" unless we have that place promised and prepared for us by Jesus!

No wonder "while in this tent, we groan." We groan, longing not to be unclothed, but safely clothed with our dwelling made by God. Our mortal must put on immortality. Our corruptible flesh must put on an incorruptible "home."

And I don't know about you, but I'm excited about seeing my forever place!"

CHAPTER 13:

WALKING WITH GOD IN THE SHADOWS

No single passage of Scripture, either Old or New Testaments, is as familiar as the one we know as "The Shepherd's Psalm." The words are as familiar as the face of an old friend, or the feeling of your child curling up in your arms, or the fragrance of a favorite meal wafting in from the kitchen.

The Twenty-Third Psalm brings us comfort in the most difficult of days. It brings us light and guidance in times of darkness and confusion. It speaks of our heads being "anointed with oil" by the shepherd, but in reality it is our souls that are anointed by His comforting Presence. We are not alone. The Shepherd walks before us.

The Psalm consists of about fifty-seven words in the Hebrew language. Not long by most counts. While the words are familiar, their meaning isn't always clear. Some of that has to do with our lack of familiarity with shepherding animals.

It is something of a mystery as we wonder why David, himself a shepherd, called to mind the imagery of God as a great Shepherd rather than as "El:" the God of angel armies, or "Yahweh-Jireh," the God of Provision. It is believed that David recited or maybe wrote these words while in hiding from those who would take his life. The words and imagery of this beloved Psalm are much older than David, though unlike Saul's armor, he wears the verses of this Hebrew song comfortably. But why did this picture come to mind, rather than those pictures of God as a mighty warrior, or strong tower, or reigning King?

Perhaps it was because, as the Holy Spirit inspired his thoughts and his pen, he really needed a shepherd. A valley had loomed large in his life. He now found himself in the midst of that shadowland.

At this time in his life David was hiding out from Saul's hitmen in an area of wilderness called *Hereth*, which in English roughly means "baked earthenware." It was hardly a place we would select from a travel brochure to visit. He didn't wish to stay there, but his escape route was unclear. He was in a place where he was unlikely to be pursued by the enemy, but he needed a reliable guide to follow who would lead him out of this wilderness experience. He needed a kind word to greet him. He needed a shepherd.

At times, we don't know how to ask for what we need. You will not journey far in life before you find yourself facing circumstances for which you have no words, and truly don't even know what you need to ask for in the moment. It is then that the "Comforter," God's Holy Spirit, meets us and speaks deep words that "cannot be uttered."

God translates our needs for us. If you have ever walked into a coffee shop and tried to order without knowing their "coded" language, you might order a medium cup of coffee with cream. And they will ask, "You mean a grande?" To which you might say "What's a grande?" They will then hand you back a "grande coffee" with a little room at the top and no cream! What have they done? They translated your need for you, put it into their language, and gently corrected your lack of information hoping you'll get it right next time! The barista knew what you needed even though you didn't know how to ask for it. God knows too. Even when our "asking" is for what we think we want or need, God can "translate" for us and get us to where we most need to be.

If you stand in a dark valley today, you too need a shepherd. With Psalm 23, God translated for you what you really needed...and really wanted most! While that may not have been your first request, or the language you used, it is what you need most. Maybe you want instant deliverance, or for God to take on and defeat your enemies.

God often hears our concerns and requests, translates our need, and gives us back what we really needed in the first place but asked for incorrectly. In the Book of Acts, a lame beggar confronted Peter and John asking them for alms...money. Not an uncommon request so near the Temple, but Peter and John had no money. They told him that. "Silver and gold we do not have, but what we do have we give (freely) to you; in the name of Jesus of Nazareth stand up and walk." And to everyone's amazement, the beggar stood and not only that, but ran and jumped and rejoiced.

They gave him what he needed, but not what he had asked them to give him...and not only that, but far more than he could have asked or imagined. He wanted money. He needed healing. Such is the grace of God. And sometimes in His grace He becomes, not a mighty warrior, but a gentle Shepherd to watch over, heal, and guide us.

He is not just any Shepherd however. David said, "The Lord is my shepherd." That is far different than saying, "The Lord is a Shepherd, or the Lord is a Great Shepherd." This little personal pronoun sets this Shepherd apart, and sets the words before us on fire.

Shepherds love the animals they keep. Their job requires, still in many places today, for them to live away from home and with the animals they cared for, at least for a time. The familiar shepherds who "kept watch over their flocks by night" in the birth narratives of Jesus were living with their sheep outside of Bethlehem.

They would live with the animals and sleep in shifts with others working with them. They would experience the same elements of heat and rain and cold and night as the animals they tended. One of the reasons shepherds were considered religious outcasts in the Middle East was the impossibility of their attending the Sabbath service. They were unclean by virtue of their outdoor life and inability to participate in ritual cleansing and they were unclean by virtue of their lack of religious piety or opportunity to make atonement for their sins.

But they knew their sheep. They knew their sheep by name and by need. They knew the ones most apt to wander off, and those most likely to steal the food from the other sheep. They knew the ones that were skittish, and likely to bolt when startled. They knew their flocks well.

In the same way, as Jesus referred to Himself as "the Great Shepherd," He added the remark "My sheep know my voice." Jesus knows His flock. He knows your weaknesses, your fears, your greatest needs. He is MY shepherd, the One Who named me and knows my name best.

And because our Shepherd knows us so well, we can say with David, "I shall not want." Now let's understand the context this was spoken in before we go further. David was likely hiding and running for his life from a toxic king who wanted him dead. Knowing the country-side as well as he did, David knew where to hide away from the search parties sent out by Saul.

He was separated from the comforts of home and the safety of family. He was not enjoying the finest of cuisine. He did not have a warm bed to sleep in, and didn't know where his next meal would come from. Though God had told him through the old prophet Samuel that he would be the next king of Israel, he certainly wasn't living like a king!

This was anything but a picture of a man living it up in the best of circumstances. And yet, he affirmed "I shall not want." That is the picture of a man, despite the worst of conditions, who found content-ment. He had what he needed. One translation renders this phrase, "He's all that I need." In the valley, David discovered that His God was not only a mighty warrior, and a great King, but also a faithful and gen-tle Shepherd guiding him when he didn't have a clue where to turn next!

That's the Shepherd we need to guide us through the valley. He is not here one day and gone the next. He lives with us, in our circumstances and even in our mess. "I will never leave you nor forsake you," Jesus promised.

The Psalmist's next affirmation is that "He makes me to lie down in green pastures." The poetic style employed would make this a phrase that re-emphasizes the previous statement. "I shall not want" and "He makes me lie down" are two ways of saying the same thing: God is an amazing Provider.

Sheep don't worry too much about having their needs met, but they are reluctant to lie down as long as their needs are unmet. In fact, sheep can be as stubborn as mules. But if you see in a photo or you witness a flock of sheep resting serenely in a pasture full of green grass, you can thank the shepherd. He has led them there, and they have had enough. Their bellies are full. The shepherd came through!

In the weeks following my wife's death, I took to the road. I needed to think, to weep, to re-organize my thinking, and to hear from the Shepherd. The word that kept coming back to me in this season of brokenness was "Be still, and know that I am God." Being still didn't work for me. I will do things, go places, study, preach...but being still didn't enter my skill set.

But seeking to obey, I secured a friend's parents cabin in the Blue Ridge mountains. Located along the rolling waters of the Toccoa River, it looked like just the place for a retreat to pray, think, write, and be still before God.

When I arrived I found that someone else was in the cabin for another night, and I was invited to stay in the lovely home of my hosts who owned the cabin. She was an interior designer, and the home was beautiful. I was told that I was to stay in a bedroom on the main floor, and after visiting a bit I retired to my temporary quarters.

Clicking on the bedside light, I noticed painted on the wall above my bed were two large iron gates. Garden gates. The first thought I had seeing it was, "My wife would love this." It gave me comfort to know I was in a place where she, too, would have been happy. But in the center of the gates were these words, "Be still and know that I am God."

It may sound strange, but in that moment I knew I was in the right place, and at the right time. I got the message! Sometimes God has to paint it on the wall for us to get it. That night, I rested for the first time since my wife's death.

Part of what I learned is this: Rest is not about a prescribed period of time. It is not about a particular place. Biblical rest never stops, because to "rest" or "cease" means to rest in a person. We "rest" in God. We never stop resting. The Book of Hebrews uses the imagery of rest to describe salvation. Rest doesn't mean to lay around and swing in a hammock, as nice as that sometimes sounds. It means to bring our needs, our struggles, our anxiety to the Lord and, in Him, find rest. "Come to Me all you who labor and are heavy laden and I will give you rest."

We do not rest *from* something...we rest *in* Someone. In Hebrew, the word for sabbath is "shavot." It was not a verb. It was a noun. It was not just a day to observe. In "shavot" we declare the Presence of God and lie down in that Presence like sheep lying in a green pasture. The sheep can rest because the Shepherd has worked! They can "be still" because a caring hand has cleared the way for their rest to be possible.

A green pasture was not just something happened upon in Israel. Most soil, even grassy areas, is covered with sharp stones and briars that would harm the sheep. So the shepherd would go ahead of them and clear the ground of stones and briars. It was then a pasture that would be safe and comfortable for the sheep to eat and rest. But not until the shepherd toiled.

We rest because God worked. We rest on the seventh day because God...not we...worked for six. And we can be still in the green pasture because the Shepherd has come to remove the stones of guilt, the pointed thorns of accusation, and allowed the green grass of grace to flourish that we might find rest for our weariness. We no longer run and seek to hide from our sin and shame. We can rest in His finished work on the cross.

But what of the phrase "He makes us lie down?" It has a sense of force to it, which you understand as useless if you've ever tried to make an animal lay down when it didn't want to rest. They bounce back up like they are spring-loaded!

The phrase is not to be interpreted literally, but figuratively as the shepherd sets the circumstances in place for rest to be possible. To "lie down" is also a rich word that does not come through fully in English translations. It was actually a word that meant, "to draw near to in rest." We would say, "snuggle up." That's not too far-fetched. Sheep would sometimes do that, much as your pet would. Especially on a cold night!

What a picture of God's sheep, us...the "sheep of His fold"...snuggling up next to our Shepherd in rest. No worry. No anxiety. Nothing chasing us causing us to panic. No more running in fear or shame. Simply resting in the Shepherd. That is His provision for those who call upon His name.

Not only does the Psalm affirm our Shepherd's care in providing green pastures, but it further tells us "He leads me beside still waters." This could bring two things to mind for a person in that part of the world.

Still waters are waters that did not startle the sheep. Phillip Keller relates that no matter how thirsty, sheep will not drink from babbling brooks or running streams of water. The water must be still. Water can be life-saving, or life-threatening.

For our twenty-fifth wedding anniversary, our church sent me and Pam off on a Hawaiian vacation. Neither of us had been, and Pam had always wanted to take a trip there. So we went.

After a couple of nights on Oahu, we flew over to Maui where we spent the rest of our time. I had only two things I wanted to do while there: I wanted to fly in a helicopter, and I wanted to scuba dive.

I bought a day with a diving company, and they came early in the morning to "train" me for our adventure in the swimming pool of our hotel. After a few perfunctory maneuvers, I was placed in a van filled with a vacationing Canadian family. I was alone since scuba diving was not preferable to a spa day for my wife.

When we got to the beach I entered the water looking like Jacques Cousteau (or Sean Connery in Thunderball...don't ask). What I did not know was that I was the only person in the van who had never been in real scuba gear before, nor in an ocean doing a dive. The Canadians and my instructor started disappearing under the surface one by one until I was alone in the blue Pacific waters. Alone, alone. So I tried to go under. I made it a couple of inches below the surface, and then attempted to suck all the air out of my tank in one gulp.

I quickly came back to the surface, ripped off my mask and started gasping for real air. Then, after calming myself, I tried it again. Again, same result. It was then, as I looked back to the beach at the tiny van we had come out of a little while before, that I realized I was in for forty-five minutes of floating on the still waters off Maui (unless I saw a shark). No way I was going back down there again!

In a few moments (in my mind-an eternity!) the instructor popped back up to the surface and said "THERE you are! Why aren't you down?" I said, "If you must know I went under twice and thought I was drowning." To which he replied, "Oooh, I forgot! First timer!"

Then, he carefully explained to me that it happens to everyone the first try and not to give up. He carefully walked me through step-by- step and afterward I experienced the joy of diving below the surface and remained under for forty minutes!

The difference: an experienced guide. A shepherd. A person who had been there and done that. The person who, in the middle of that experience, I trusted most.

We all find ourselves in circumstances at times that are perhaps unfamiliar or in some way threatening to us. Sheep found themselves constantly in need of a shepherd or they would die of thirst.

Frankly some of us would prefer death to having to trust! We have a Shepherd Who stands ready to "lead us beside still waters" into a life of "living water" flowing from within. But it requires us first to trust the Good Shepherd Who laid down His life for His sheep.

And sometimes the still waters can become very dangerous. A body of water took center stage in several stories as the Gospels tell us about Jesus. This particular "sea" or "lake" had three names: The Sea of Galilee, the Sea of Tiberius, and Lake Genessaret. I have sailed on the Sea of Galilee, (and bought a shirt to prove it)!

Our crew and passengers were fortunate. The sea was not choppy that day. It was some of the most placid water you will ever sail when not being visited by a storm. But storms come there frequently.

The Sea of Galilee is the lowest fresh water body on earth at almost seven hundred feet below sea level. It is surrounded by the hills of Galilee, stretched over a quarter of a mile above the lake and to the east sits the plateau known as the Golan Heights. The mountains of Lebanon (with Mount Hermon at almost 10,000 feet) are located to the north. The desert winds, the breezes from the Mediterranean and the mountain air collide often creating ferocious storms on the otherwise peaceful waters.

As we cruised along the waters enjoying the warm early morning air, I remembered the Gospel story about the disciples enjoying a sleepy evening cruise across those very waters. Suddenly, the sea grew choppy and then one of these characteristic storms blew up, threatening to tear the boat apart.

The disciples, who had just watched Jesus perform a number of miracles, suddenly panicked and cried out for their lives. And where was Jesus? Asleep in the bottom of the boat!

Jesus won't let you drown, whether you're over your head in a circumstance you can't understand or going down for the third time in a storm not of your making.

Jesus simply came to the top deck on the ship and said to the waters, to the wind, to no one in particular, "Be still." And the winds and waves grew placid as suddenly as the storm had blown up. It left in its wake twelve startled, amazed and soaking wet disciples. They had just seen God on their ship taking control of a life-threatening storm and winning!

He is the Great Shepherd Who leads us beside the still waters. The Hebrew phrase calls these "still" waters "waters of rest and relaxation." Only the Great Shepherd can turn the frightening into a holiday; the threatening into a treat. He leads us beside the still waters.

And even in the storms, He stands always ready to "restore our soul."

CHAPTER 14:

FROM THE SHADOWS TO RESTORATION

Home restoration shows are a hot ticket on cable TV these days. HGTV and TLC are filled with them. Some of the most highly viewed TV shows on right now focus on a couple, or a company, that purchases and fixes up old houses and then flips them for profit. We are fascinated as a culture by these shows.

I'm sure there is a perfectly good entertainment-related answer for the question of why is this is the case. But I think that whatever the entertainment value may be, there is something hopeful about a show that takes a house that rodents would complain about and in the span of less than thirty minutes turns it into a profit-maker.

We love the stories of people who were rejected and cast out by society coming back, usually through ingenuity and pulling themselves up by their own bootstraps, and making good. The reality is that the Bible is filled with such stories of redemption, but it is not them pulling themselves up. God is doing the work of restoration in their lives. And some great stories are still happening right now in fact!

In the Twenty-Third Psalm, we are told that one of the many things the Shepherd does for us is "restore our souls." We almost consider this little phrase an attachment to a larger thought, and don't consider it's power when we simply let it stand alone.

We lingered beside the still waters, the "waters of rest and re-laxation" as the last chapter concluded. But now we pick up and move further with this phrase. What exactly does it mean to have our souls "restored?"

Let's first state emphatically that salvation is not a remodeling project. This is not in any way stating that we are just like a run-down house that needs new carpet and a fresh coat of paint and a few flowers planted outside and we're as good as new.

No, the picture the Bible paints of mankind's condition, ravaged by sin as we ALL are, is one of absolute devastation and destruction. I have visited a few times in Florida's panhandle and seen areas close to "ground zero" of Hurricane Michael's 2018 entry into the United States. Devastation is not even a word that covers the utter destruction of the hardest hit areas. And to show up with a truck advertising "Home Restoration" would be a mockery. In some places only a concrete slab is left of their home. Nothing is left to restore!

Sin totally destroys all it touches. And our path to righteousness before God is not a restoration project. We aren't fixer-uppers. We have nothing. There is nothing to even start over with. We are ruined. We need a new life for salvation to be effective. Only God can bring that, and only then through the substitutionary death of Jesus Christ for our sin.

But sometimes, even after salvation, there are parts of our being that have not fully come back or been restored. In Romans 12:1-2, Paul tells us to let our minds be renewed by the Word of God. That's a call for those who have come to Jesus to begin to think like what they now are! Our minds need to be renewed; "restored" to use our word in the Psalm.

We need to be released from old hurts and woundings, anger and hatred, habits and hang ups, our ill temper and our profane mouth. We need to be released from bitterness, and regret, failure and guilt. These things are indications that sin is still trying to work it's way back into our soul, and we must cooperate with God through the power of His Spirit in stopping it's onslaught.

The word that is used in the Psalm can even mean, "He brings me back to life." Sometimes life wears us down, or even wears us out. It may be physical exhaustion, emotional exhaustion, depletion due to a stressful relationship, depression, or any variety of stress. All of them leave us with souls needing to be restored.

Our Great Shepherd promises this as part of what He will do for those Who walk with Him. The "sheep of His pasture" are promised restoration!

He is a faithful Shepherd Who provides for us...even in the valley. Somehow, in the shadowland that can be frightening and deep and dark, He "leads us in paths of righteousness." He can make the darkness bright.

A friend shared with me the insight that sometimes the "paths of righteousness" can lead us in the dark valley. We cannot believe that walking in paths of righteousness will inevitably lead us into sunny days, and plentiful grass. Sometimes, as Moses learned, the path of righteousness leads to the desert before it leads to the land of promise. Three displaced and relocated Hebrew young men- Shadrach, Meschach and Abednego -learned that the paths of righteousness led to a fiery furnace, and Daniel learned that it led to the lion's pit.

And of course, for Jesus, walking the path of righteouness for God's glory led to a cross. That alone should give us pause to think. David was following God's leadership as he fled for his life from Saul's anger. The "paths of righteousness" for David led to a cave, cut off from family, friends, and home.

Sometimes, the paths of righteousness deposit us directly into the "valley of the shadow of death." It does not say they lead us to easy paths, paths of abundance or paths that are not fraught with danger. It is simply enough that He leads us even in that place. Elsewhere the

Psalmist wrote, *"Where can I go from Your Spirit, or where can I flee from Your Presence?"*

I don't remember much about my childhood Bible school experiences except I know I was there...every year. I remember some of the craft projects, especially one that involved melting down an LP record (probably a Beatles album) and bending the still-warm plastic into a bowl-like shape. I was proud to take it home to my parents. It was something no home in the 60s should be without: an ashtray! (Nothing like ashtrays being mass produced by child labor in a Baptist church I guess).

But I also well remember this. I remember standing in neat rows with my peers, both boys and girls, in clean white shirts. We stood at attention for our "commencement" service and flanked by the American and the Christian flags, we sang. Loudly. The song I most remember singing is a hymn we have long since stopped singing. It said,

> *"He leadeth me o' blessed thought,*
> *Oh words with heavenly comfort fraught*
> *What ere I do, where ere I be*
> *Still tis God's hand that leadeth me."*
>
> —Joseph Gilmore

I sang that song as if I believed it, because I believe I truly did, as much as my nine-year old mind would let me recall that experience. It has followed me in my memory for over half a century. Somewhere in that crowd of white blouses the girls were wearing for graduation stood my wife, singing the same song at the same time. Though only eight or nine, she had the same memory. We sang it like we meant it, because we did!

And He has led me. He has led us. And He still leads me today. I have never backed away from my confidence that, even in the valley of the shadow, He has led me. "By His own hand He leadeth me."

A Walk Through the Valley

Recently I missed a wedding rehearsal. I didn't mean to. The venue was not at our church campus and therefore I relied on my GPS to guide me to this new location. What I was unaware of was there were two venues very similar in name, and they were in something of a war, competing for billing on Google.

I loaded the directions for the address Google gave me, and headed off...approximately forty five miles in the wrong direction! Ten or fifteen minutes before the rehearsal was to begin, I called the bride and said, "I have just turned onto a dirt road that leads off into the horizon. Am I on the right road?" And she said, "Yes there's a dirt road."

So I continued on through the dust and into the horizon, riding on like some cowboy into the sunset. Forty five minutes. In the wrong direction. I arrived at a ranch, and after waiting for over five minutes for someone to answer my page at the gate, a gentleman arrived on a golf cart only to inform me "yes we do weddings. No we aren't doing one today."

I'm not sure I learned any deep spiritual lesson from that experience. I tried to think of something-I truly did. But nothing occurred to me. It was just one of those "ended up at the wrong place thinking it was the right one" experiences. Even with technology it's easy to get off the path.

Let me put a sharper point on this. Sometimes the paths where God leads us take us to pleasant places; beautiful scenery, plentiful provisions, great jobs, happy families, good health. Certainly we will give glory to God for His wisdom in leading us to those places.

But we must equally be prepared to give Him glory when our paths lead, not to places WE would see as "right," but to places God sees as right for us...for the time being. And sometimes that path leads us into the valley the Psalmist is talking about.

What is the "valley of the shadow of death?" What does this really mean? It actually says "a valley of deep darkness," or "tzalamut," which was a region where few had ever gone before. Somewhere in the years since the Old Testament has been translated, it seemed good to put "death" in the phraseology to seek to clarify the ominous nature of this word.

It's a shadowy place. By nature, it creates fear in those who must pass through. As a shepherd, David had gone through "tzalamut" before. He was no stranger to the dark places since, as a shepherd boy, he had slept under the night sky with his sheep.

And even in the night, shadows can appear. A shadow is always an indication that something is MAKING the shadow. Shadows do not just appear for no reason. There are shadowy things that threaten us, and certainly death is one of those.

A young father had just days before experienced the death of his wife after a battle with cancer. Two identically dressed little girls sat quietly in the back seat, neither absorbing this untimely visit to a cemetery to bury their mother. The father struggled with how to put what was happening into words his precious little girls could understand.

Suddenly a large semi truck drove passed them, momentarily obscuring the sunlight and shading the car. And the father had an inspiration. Breaking the silence in the car he asked the girls a question. He said, "Girls, would you rather be run over by that big truck that just drove past us, or by it's shadow?" "Well, the shadow Daddy...because it can't hurt you." "Exactly!" He continued, "your Mommy knew Jesus well and Jesus knew her. So when death came to her in the hospital, it was just the shadow of death that came. Your Mommy is alive in Heaven right now! Death didn't hurt her, because a shadow doesn't hurt!"

There's a Psalm that has become very precious to me personally. It is Psalm 91, a favorite of many. I began to take comfort in it before my wife's death, and continue to draw strength from meditating on it's reality.

He who dwells in the shelter of the Most High
Will abide in the shadow of the Almighty.
I will say to the Lord, "My refuge and my fortress,
My God, in whom I trust!"
For it is He who delivers you from the snare of the trapper
And from the deadly pestilence.
He will cover you with His pinions,
And under His wings you may seek refuge;
His faithfulness is a shield and bulwark.

I was traveling through a part of the country in 2017 during the Great Eclipse. Actually I was driving through what was known as "the path of totality;" the optimal place to see it. Some of my routes went through places where the eclipse could be seen unobstructed. People were literally coming from all over the world to find a spot near there to see it.

Those who witnessed it personally (I was not one) tell us that, while the area grew noticeably darker during the eclipse, the larger out-shining of the suns rays still provided some light. Even in a moment where a perfect shadow sought to quench the light of the sun, it was in-effective in completely doing so.

When the shadowy times come to our lives, and we find our-selves walking through "tzalamut," whether our shadow is caused by the passing of a loved one or the loss of a job, the diagnosis of cancer or the arrest of a child, remember two things. These shadow times can seem overwhelming in their finality.

First, remember that as a child of God you dwell under a shadow much larger than the one that is seeking to intimidate you with fear and anxiety and dread. You are "abiding under the shadow of His wings." The shadow that God casts is the shadow of wings that cover anything that may seek to terrify you in the night, or take you down in the day. And the "shadow of His wings" is much larger than the shadow of any-thing that may come your way.

Secondly remember the promise of Psalm 23. "I will fear no evil for You are with me." There is a subtle but important shift in pronouns at this part of the Psalm. The words "You" and "Your" begin to be used, as though God were standing right beside you. "You" anoint my head with oil. "You" prepare a table before me.

His shadow is bigger; His Presence is greater than anything you will ever encounter in the valley. "I will fear no evil, for You are with me." And if the Shepherd is with us, we can journey on, for we don't lie down in this valley.

We walk through it.

CHAPTER 15:

BEYOND THE SHADOWS TO OUR HOME

Nothing in the Word of God is accidental. Even the placement and ordering of the books of the Bible have a significance that most believe was God-directed. The mention of the comfort of the rod and staff the Shepherd brought is important right here.

The shepherd's staff in Biblical times was a two-fold instrument. It could be used as a staff to protect and direct and even rescue the sheep on one end; leading them to the water they needed for instance or using the crook at one end to pull a wandering sheep back. The rod was, on the other end, a deadly weapon that could be wielded against an enemy approaching.

The Great Shepherd uses His rod and His staff, the living Word of God, both as a source of our protection and direction as well as a weapon against the enemy. It could be a deadly weapon, or an instrument of guidance and protection for the flock. It comforted them.

The Biblical shepherds would do something else with their staff, however. When a significant event took place on their journey, they would etch the story into their staff. As David experienced his encounter with a lion and a bear, these were etched onto his staff as a written testimony to God's protection. It became a record for God's faithfulness in the shepherd's life. We don't know, but it seems certain

David would never have parted with this precious instrument.

God writes what is true about you onto His staff. He etches your identity onto His Shepherd's staff. Much of this is already recorded in the Book we call the Bible. It speaks the truth about what God thinks about you; what God believes about you; what He has done for you to show His love and care and protection.

Sadly other stories have also been etched into our minds. They become toxic memories the enemy can use to torment us with shame, anxiety and despair. The negative memories we house actually shape our brain through neural channels that are constantly changing. They can actually change your body chemistry and physiological makeup!

You are going to believe either God's stories and truth about you, or your own. David had much to overcome within himself, erasing stories and innuendo and gossip that surrounded him. Saul considered him a traitor to the king. Many rabbis speculate that David was the child of an illicit relationship, which may explain why he wasn't invited in with the other brothers when Saul visited looking for the next king (1 Samuel 16)

David had to decide which narrative he was going to embrace, and which he was going to carve into his staff. So do you. Those stories about you and what your Shepherd has done to lead and sometimes carry you through the valleys become the foundation of a hopeful and grace-full future.

The Great Shepherd's rod and staff will comfort you.

A Table Prepared

It was believed historically that David's time of wandering in the wilderness of Hereth was a time that took a toll on him physically. Food would have been scarce in such a barren place, and hunting would have been dangerous with Saul's soldiers searching.

So naturally, when you're hungry, food is foremost on your mind. David meditated on a table set, no doubt with many of his favorite foods. But something at this table was out of place: an enemy.

Fast forward several hundred years and another table was set...this time a Passover meal with Jesus and His twelve disciples seated. And as they were preparing to eat the first course, and enjoying the appetizer of bread dipped in a date-based sauce on the table, Jesus made an announcement: "One of you will betray me."

Each man immediately turned eyes inward (all but the enemy of course) and asked, "Lord is it me? Am I the traitor?" Even the betrayer asked the question aloud to cover himself. Jesus said, "It is one of you whose hand is with mine in the bowl.".

Now we don't know if Jesus and Judas had dipped their bread in the sop at the same moment. That would have made it very clear who the traitor was. But it was in that moment the enemy was told to leave. Jesus whispered to Judas, "Go do what you must do."

And Judas left. He left because there are those times, those meals, those moments of intimacy, when the enemy gets to watch but he cannot enter in. Judas never got to enjoy the intimacy that Jesus and the remaining eleven men knew that night. The enemy can watch,but not ever enjoy the bliss that fellow with Jesus and with the Body of Christ.

David said, "You prepare a table before me in the presence of my enemies." This was an invitation, not just for the food, but into the deepest level of intimacy that could be shared in Middle Eastern bedouin life. The question that lingers over this is, "Why?" Why would an enemy be invited to a meal?

Well one possible answer is that God wishes to show the enemy his care for those who love Him. He wants to demonstrate the riches of His grace for those who love and follow Him. He wants the enemy to see...but not enjoy...the table prepared. He is invited as a spectator, but not as a participant.

David was enjoying a feast in his wilderness hideout. It was a feast set in the presence of his enemy...a feast that Saul could never enjoy. A feast of the fullness of God's grace for Him. It was a feast of intimacy with God Himself. David feasted on that meat that Jesus spoke of...bread that you do not know...as He shared with the Samaritan woman at the well in John's Gospel. It is a feast that is set knowing that man does not live by bread alone, but by every Word that proceeds from the mouth of God.

A Discovery channel special discussed the behavior of African elephants. When a newborn is born into the herd, they instinctively know this little one must be protected by all. It cannot see yet, and it's small body and temporary blindness make it easy prey for a predator.

When an invader is spotted, the herd begins to stomp their large feet as they surround the little one. This lets any would-be invader know that it risks this meal at the cost of being flattened by their large feet and heavy bodies. The enemy can see the meal waiting...but no way will it risk it's life for a quick lunch. So it wisely turns the other way.

So does your enemy. God has set the table for you, His child. The enemy may circle and watch you enjoying your meal, God's grace, your life in Him. But he will not be allowed to invade the camp. He knows the cost will be great if he does.

He witnesses a meal he cannot enjoy. A table is prepared in the presence of the enemy. But for those Who trust themselves to the Great Shepherd, the table awaits!

The Overflowing Cup

Phillip Keller, author of *A Shepherd Looks at the 23rd Psalm* among other books, helps us with insights into Biblical and more modern practices of nomadic life. The next two phrases in the Psalm are based on nomadic practices still engaged in today to a degree.

What does it mean to have your head anointed with oil? In the world of shepherds, hospitality was and still is important. Comfortable lodging does not exist for some. It would not be uncommon for a shepherd or his entire family to enter your camp and request lodging or a meal.

If the man of the camp was willing for them to stay, the first thing that would be done would be pouring oil over their heads. This would be the same oil the shepherd may use on the sheep to kill parasites and lice. It was a fragrant oil, and provided some degree of cleansing and hygiene for the guests visiting (they would not often have access to water or soap) and the oil made them, for a moment at least, to feel (and smell) cleaner. It prepared them and made them acceptable.

As a side note, it also killed lice which not only the sheep would acquire, but people too. The oil made certain that other "visitors" did not remain behind after the guests had left! So it served a cleansing and hygienic purpose, but also a medicinal one.

But if you were allowed to attend the meal in the camp, you would be given a cup of wine at the closing of the meal. If your presence had not been appreciated and the host did not want you to stay overnight, the cup handed to the head of the visitors would be half full. That was a way of saying, "Nice to meet you...now get going."

However if the evening was pleasant, and the conversation enjoyable, when it was time to retire for the night the host would hand the guest a cup, not half-full, but brimming over! An overflowing cup was an invitation to linger...to stay...to make yourself at home.

No doubt both of these customs were in mind as David hummed and meditated and wrote the words of this Psalm inspired by God's Spirit. He found God to be a welcoming host, anointing his head...preparing him to be able to sit in the Presence of the Lord...cleansing him of the stench of death and sin, healing him of his diseases...but more than that. He felt that God was offering him a cup overflowing with grace and the invitation to stay in His Presence.

David was, according to some historians and Biblical scholars, an outcast son. The "runt" of the litter, small of stature...David was sentenced to sheep tending for his father while his brothers went off to war. David would have no Medal of Honor pinned on his chest for keeping sheep.

It seems logical that David was probably not a full brother to Jesse's sons. He was treated as though he was unwanted by his father and his brothers. And certainly when the prophet came to anoint the next king of Israel, it never occurred to David's father Jesse to invite him for consideration.

And yet, in spite of that rejection, David had not been rejected by God. He was, in fact, chosen by Samuel the prophet...and prophets identified and made kings...to be the next reigning king of Israel. He was anointed there in the presence of his family with a flask of oil poured over his head, flowing down into his beard and clothing his body in fragrant and spiritually symbolic oil. Oil, in the Old Testament, was frequently a visible sign of God's Spirit clothing an individual for a specific task for a specific time.

No doubt, David was reflecting on that experience. "You chose me, God. You called me to be king. You singled me out by anointing my head with oil." He was probably remembering the details of that day in the not too distant past.

It is not hard for us to make the connection to the One Who came in the bloodline of David Who was likewise cast out and rejected by His own family, even though He was God's chosen One...the One Who would be king. We see this picture clearly being worked out in the narrative of David's life.

The rejected. The outlier. The outcast. The damaged. These are the ones who will receive a welcome and hospitality at the Father's tent and table. They are the ones God chooses to anoint with His cleansing and fragrant oil and they are the ones made fit for His Presence by the blood of Jesus. And they are the ones who enjoy the table prepared for them in the presence of the enemy. None who will come to him will be turned away.

We come to Him covered with sin's stench, sores, diseases, guilt and shame. And He receives us with the hospitality of grace. He anoints us with His oil of gladness, and clothes us with His own robe of righteousness. He sets a table for the undesirable, the unacceptable, in the presence of the enemy.

And He serves them His grace.

Pursued by Goodness and Mercy

The Psalm ends with two phrases that are powerful affirmations of faith. One is of a present and continuing pursuit by the good things of God. The other is a promise of an amazing destination.

Remember again that as these words were being written and sung by the shepherd-king they were not being sung from the parapet of a castle or a courtyard filled with flowers. These were words sung in the "valley of the shadow of death." David sang these words in the shadows.

That's where they're most needed. When our steps have entered a shadowy place: sitting while powerful chemo drugs course into our veins, walking into a funeral home to make preparations for the burial of a spouse, or signing the final papers on a divorce as our life mate walks away from their marriage vows. The shadows.

In the valley occasionally a sheep would wander away. This is the concern in the parable of the shepherd who left the ninety-nine to pursue the wandering one. The lost one wandered into a valley. The threat in such a place was great. Rescue must come quickly.

I don't know about you, but I'm glad God doesn't write us off when we wander away. He chases us down with "goodness and mercy," and will doggedly pursue us all the days of our life. In His mercy He draws and calls and speaks our name. In goodness He gives what we do not deserve.

And at the end, He takes us into His home, where we will "dwell in the house of the Lord forever." If you long for a home you can't quite seem to find on Earth, it's because you were meant for another one...an eternal one...that you never have to leave.

That was the dream of the Middle Eastern nomad...and today it may be your dream as well. Dreams can come true when you're under the watchful care of the Great Shepherd.

And you can trust Him to lead you beyond the valley.

CHAPTER 16:

A GLIMPSE OF OUR HEAVENLY HOME

I have taken several international trips in my lifetime. The longest was from the United States to Dubai in the United Arab Emirates. I actually spent quite a bit of time preparing for that fourteen hour overnight stretch in the air.

Having never been to the desert before, I continually checked the weather map to see what the weather wold be like while there for two weeks. What does one wear in the desert? Then there were the concerns about passports, since we were entering a foreign country.

Internet issues were a concern, as were power supplies for phones and tablets. Adapters for electricity were also required. Did I bring the right ones? Which books should I bring to read during the time away? Did I pack enough clothing? The mission organization we were traveling for provided a long checklist, including a mandatory life insurance form and a sobering "expatriation" form to give permission to transport your body out of the Saudi Arabian emirotes in case you died while on the trip!

I read for weeks ahead of time about the people, the customs, the culture and the history of Dubai and the UAE. Partly I wanted to be knowledgeable about these things so as not to offend. But mostly, I was excited! I couldn't wait to take the trip and see this incredible part of the world. I wondered what the people would be like, how the food would taste, how the city would look. The Burj, then the world's tallest hotel, was opening the week we were there.

All this was for a two-week (ten-day) trip overseas. I wasn't going off on military deployment, or to work somewhere for six months. But my two-week foray into this country preoccupied my thinking for months beforehand.

It makes me wonder sometimes how much thought we really give to our eternal destination that will be, well, PERMANENT! Many contemporary believers seldom give a thought to the home waiting for them when the pathway of this life ends.

And it will end. The Bible assures us that "It is appointed to man once to die..." (Hebrews 9:7) and then your eternal destination is all there will be to think about. Paul tells us in Colossians that we are to "(continually) set our minds on heavenly things..." (Colossians 3:1). It sounds like there is certainly an advantage to spending time on earth making preparation for this trip.

Becoming Heavenly Minded

So what do you think about heaven? Or do you much? Do you have a mind that's prepared, and a heart that's shaped for the place that will be your eternal home?

Most people have some ideas about heaven, though they are usually informed by confusing cultural ideas that we cut and paste from our music and movies and a smidgen of superstition or a dash of spiritualism or philosophy. And when we see the tepid or downright odd portrayals of Heaven in our media today, it's no wonder more of us aren't excited about the prospect of going there.

If Heaven is walking through a multi-colored psychedelic landscape that looks like the backdrop of an abstract art painting or a place, as even some who claim to be Christian believe, that is one unending church service without Starbucks coffee, then no wonder we aren't ex-

142

cited to go.

But I think these misconceptions of our eternal home are exactly what the enemy of our soul wants us to believe. If we believe these cartoonish and unrealistic portrayals of Heaven we will not live with our eyes fixed on spiritual things "where Christ is seated." We will not sacrifice much if we have no clear understanding of the rewards awaiting the faithful life. And we won't work any harder to convince our lost or unchurched friends and neighbors to want to go to Heaven than we do to convince them to come to church on Sundays.

We are far from the understanding held by the earliest believers in the New Testament church who welcomed martyrdom because they knew Heaven awaited them. But to have a half-true, anemic view of Heaven is deadly to the progress of the Kingdom and to the building up of our faith. Jesus died on earth so we could gain Heaven eternally. He must have thought it was something worth paying the price so we could gain it!

Our Citizenship in Heaven

I have a US Passport that says right on it that I'm a citizen of the United States of America, complete with a flag waving in the background. But I am actually a person with a dual citizenship. When I became a follower of Christ, the records of Heaven were changed and I became a citizen of a Heavenly kingdom. (Philippians 3:20)

As an earthly citizen of the United States, I am accorded the privileges and freedoms associated with that citizenship. I didn't earn them...I was born into them. As I honor the rules and laws of our nation, those unearned privileges continue to be mine if I don't forfeit the privilege.

Likewise my citizenship in Heaven is also unearned and undeserved. But I stive to live in such a way that I honor the laws of my true and eternal home, and do it as though I live there now. Our citizenship in Heaven does not just become active or "kick in" when we die and go there. It is in place now, even though we aren't there just yet.

My privileges of US citizenship did not change just because I was spending time in a country not a part of the United States. I was still accorded those privileges even though I was not "home." The United States Embassy assured that for me. And as Heavenly citizens, we receive the privileges now of being a part of the people of God living as ambassadors in a foreign land.

I think about this almost every time I look at my passport. "This world is not my home...I'm just a `passing through" as the old song reminds us. My citizenship is now in Heaven, not "one day will be." (Philippians 3:20). But *now* I belong to a Heavenly country.

What Will Heaven Be?

So then what will greet us when we arrive in Heaven? I can assure you there will not be a haggard old fisherman named Peter standing at the pearly gates with a clipboard ready to "check you in" to your eternal accommodations.

Your entry into Heaven was secured at Calvary's cross by Jesus. Receiving this gift by grace while still living on Planet Earth is the only entree you need. His blood is the full payment. "For we were not redeemed by perishable things, but with the spotless blood of a lamb." (1 Peter 1:18)

So that still leaves with questions: What will we see? What will we do? What will it be like? Will we know anyone around us? Will our deceased family members come to greet us? How exactly will our first experience in Heaven begin?

Sadly, and I make this statement unscientifically, more Christians know the details of Hell than the details of their Heavenly home. That is the fault of preachers now and through the years, and even behind that of theologians who have written thick and voluminous and brilliant works of theology with seldom or only a scant few pages offered about our home in Heaven.

But as I mentioned earlier, when your loved one is nearing their departure for that place or you yourself are preparing imminently for it, you become an eager student of the subject. What does the Bible teach us about Heaven? Why would God not want us to know about this exciting place where we will spend eternity with Him and in resurrected bliss with our loved ones gone before?

Well let's ask someone who has been there and come back to tell about it!

A Heavenly Visitation

The Book of Revelation, arguably one of the most important and most mistranslated books in our canon of Scripture, begins in a bleak and barren location. The Isle of Patmos, off the coast of present-day Turkey, was little more than a barren rock in the middle of the Aegean Sea.

It was used by Rome to relocate prisoners who were too difficult to execute because of political considerations. So they were usually left there to die by disease or exposure or starvation or to be killed by other prisoners. Rome could then keep their hands clean.

There, alone and perhaps walking along the beach listening to the sound of ocean waves, John heard an unusual sound. He describes this encounter in Revelation 1:

Then I turned to see the voice that was speaking to me, and on turning I saw seven golden lampstands, and in the midst of the lampstands one like a son of man, clothed with a long robe and with a golden sash around his chest. The hairs of his head were white, like white wool, like snow. His eyes were like a flame of fire, his feet were like burnished bronze, refined in a furnace, and his voice was like the roar of many waters. In his right hand he held seven stars, from his mouth came a sharp two-edged sword, and his face was like the sun shining in full strength.

John saw Jesus, who was described as "one like a son of man" clothed with a long robe and a gold sash. This was an incredible visitation. John knew Jesus well. He was there on Patmos being persecuted for "the Word of the Lord and his testimony" to Jesus. But this appearing, this "revelation" was different than the last time He saw Jesus on earth. This was Jesus glorified...shining, glowing, eyes burning, white-haired and feet of bronze.

John's only response was to fall at His feet in adoration and worship. From there, we read as John begins to receive the messages from the One Who stood in the midst of the golden lampstands...challenging, chastising, correcting, affirming and encouraging the seven churches in Asia Minor. (Revelation 2-3).

But if that were not enough, John was about to be taken to the next level in this face-to-face meeting with Jesus. He was about to be taken into the throne room of Heaven itself!

An Invitation to the Throne

The Bible is abundantly clear and unwavering on this reality, that to be "absent from the body is present with the Lord." (2 Corinthians 5:6, 8). There is no period of waiting, of atoning in purgatory, of "soul sleep" or of reincarnation to "try to do better next time."

Pastor and author Randy Alcorn noted that, worldwide, "3 people die every second, 180 every minute, and 11,000 every hour. If the Bible is right, that means 250,000 leave this life and open their eyes in either Heaven or hell every day."

When our bodies fail and our "tents" fold up, we will come immediately into the place where our eternity will begin. For those who have rejected Christ willfully and continually in this life, an eternity of separation from God, from light and from hope awaits. Eternity for them will be one despairing and tormenting experience after the other in that place prepared for "the devil and his angels."

Believers come into the Lord's presence. And....then what?

What would that look like- to close your eyes in death on the earth and open them in Heaven? Do you imagine yourself surrounded by waiting loved ones? Or perhaps you'll be floating on a beautiful, crystal-clear body of water, or maybe suspended on a cloud. Maybe you'll hear soothing, ethereal angelic harps. The good news is God does not make us wonder. In this passage of Scripture we are told exactly what is happening in Heaven from the moment we arrive.

Our First Day in Heaven

We first of all have an immediate summons to the King's throne. That is what John experienced in Revelation Chapter 4. He was called into the presence of the Lord Almighty. An angelic escort explained what was happening, but John was simply lost in awe and wonder at the incredible things he was seeing. The worship service had already begun and it was amazing to behold!

After this I looked, and behold, a door standing open in heaven! And the first voice, which I had heard speaking to me like a trumpet, said, "Come up here, and I will show you what must take place after this." At once I was in the Spirit, and behold, a throne stood in heaven, with one seated on the throne. And he who sat there had the appearance of jasper and carnelian, and around the throne was a rainbow that had the appearance of an emerald. Around the throne were twenty-four thrones, and seated on the thrones were twenty-four elders, clothed in white garments, with golden crowns on their heads. From the throne came flashes of lightning, and rumblings[a] and peals of thunder, and before the throne were burning seven torches of fire, which are the seven spirits of God, and before the throne there was as it were a sea of glass, like crystal.And around the throne, on each side of the throne, are four living creatures, full of eyes in front and behind: the first living creature like a lion, the second living creature like an ox, the third living creature with the face of a man, and the fourth living creature like an eagle in flight. And the four liv-

*ing creatures, each of them with six wings, are full of eyes all around
and within, and day and night they never cease to say,*
> *"Holy, holy, holy, is the Lord God Almighty,*
> *who was and is and is to come!"*
>   —(Revelation 4:1-8 ESV)

Though he reported being in the spirit, it was nevertheless real
and not a dream or hallucination. These things were actually happening
to John. He wasn't napping on the beach when Jesus appeared. He was
wide awake in worship, "in the Spirit on the Lord's Day." And I do not
think it is incorrect to understand that the things he experienced as described in Revelation 4-5 still continue to happen today! He was not
having a prophetic vision of some far-off day when worship around the
throne was happening like he was experiencing. He was entering an on-
going worship experience that is continuous.

Before the Throne of God We Stand

In his book *Letters to the Churches*, Francis Chan writes,
*This section begins with a majestic picture of God on His throne. The
scene is busy and intense: the four living creatures are declaring His
holiness, the seven spirits of God are blazing, myriads of angels are
praising Jesus with loud voices, and the twenty-four elders are flat on
their faces while laying their crowns before Him.*

It's an astonishing thought to me. I often imagine the reality of
the experience that my wife, and my parents and other family members
are having as they behold this scene face -to- face. Right now. It makes
worship an exciting prospect to know that as I join my voice now in
worship, I join the chorus of those who forever will proclaim:

Worthy is the Lamb that was slain to receive honor and glory…

This should make every earthly worship encounter a blessed

foretaste of what is to come. And we are supposed to long for this Heavenly experience ourselves! It makes our petty complaints about what we like or don't like about worship in a church service sound like childish and self-absorbed immaturity.

Lifting our eyes to Heavenly places purifies us here and now. I want to be counted among those who will proclaim the worth of the Lamb now by faith. In that day I will proclaim His worth because I see Him face-to-face.

And whenever the living creatures give glory and honor and thanks to him who is seated on the throne, who lives forever and ever, the twenty-four elders fall down before him who is seated on the throne and worship him who lives forever and ever. They cast their crowns before the throne, saying,

> *"Worthy are you, our Lord and God,*
> *to receive glory and honor and power,*
> *for you created all things,*
> *and by your will they existed and were created."*
> —Revelation 4:9

We must continually search our own hearts. Is it truly our desire to be included in that number? Not the number of those who want to claim their "mansion" or walk on streets of gold. If your view of Heaven is locked in to an idea of a blissful eternity that would be just as good if Jesus weren't there, then there's a great chance that you are living deceived by wishful thinking.

Unending Worship

Not infrequently I will have people ask me, "Pastor what do you think my loved one is doing in Heaven right now?" I have endured with some degree of pain eulogies in funeral services that fantasize about Dad being up in Heaven fishing right now in an eternally stocked bass lake, since "he wasn't much for going to church when he was alive." Or Mom is taking care of the most beautiful flower garden anyone ever saw. Or in one instance which I had to correct after it was spoken, "Well my Daddy is probably up in Heaven enjoying a few beers with his buddies that went on before him." Ahem. That's not happening.

Let me gently but truthfully answer this question. I say "gently" because I need to correct some un-Biblical misconceptions that we may hold. If what we are seeing in the Book of Revelation 4 and 5 are describing a present and ongoing experience, then this is what I believe: I believe our loved ones have never left that amazing worship taking place around the throne!

I've been in several worship experiences and other times of personal prayer and moments when God showed up. Heaven, quite literally, seemed to come down in power and reality. And this in an environment where sin is still present and our worship far from perfect.

And even so, I didn't want to leave. Sometimes I didn't want to move. You couldn't drag me away if you wanted to. My Father is in the room! I'm not going anywhere!

Yet this is not some grinding, endless church service that you couldn't wait to escape as a child (or, an adult)! There is a glory to coming immediately into the presence of the Lord in this place where He is being unceasingly worshiped.

The images of Heaven that we have before us in Revelation Chapters 4 and 5 are different from those in Revelation 21 and 22. That's because they are different! The intermediate state of those who are now with the Lord following their passing from this earth is different in detail, in purpose, and in activity.

"So Pastor Tim," you may ask, "are you saying you believe Heaven will change from the way it is right now?" I absolutely believe some aspects of it will. God's ultimate plan is not to pull off some rescue operation to get us off the planet. His plan is to recreate the Heavens and the Earth that we now know, corrupted by sin, and make it new and then put us back on it to live forever! That's where the final Heaven will be; not in some disembodied existence somewhere up in the clouds.

Furthermore, Heaven cannot be separated from God. It is not a place where God comes and goes. Heaven is where God is. If God is absent, Heaven doesn't exist. So when we read in the following chapters about the New Jerusalem descending onto the New Earth, the city is the place where God chooses to dwell. He doesn't have to dwell there. No temple and no city or for that matter, no planet can contain Him. But He chooses to dwell with us in the renewed Heavens and Earth. In fact, part of the reason it is renewed is so He can dwell there in His holiness and splendor! It will be His chosen sanctuary, where He can forever meet with resurrected humanity. "And the dwelling of God shall be with man."

But the primary purpose of Heaven now, according to the chapters before us seems to be focused on the worship of the Lamb taking place around the throne. In every sense of the word, those who are there can see, talk, think, ask questions, interact with each other, and even intercede for those on earth. They are alive! More alive than they were before!

They have emotion, form and size, the ability to pray and offer incense. They exist without pain or any sense of sorrow or regret, loneliness or grief. They are, well, in Heaven! God is there. The Lamb is present and on the throne. (Revelation 6:19-21)

Paul gave expression to his understanding of this when he said in Philippians 1:21 that he "had a desire to depart and be with Christ, which is better by far." Paul had seen a glimpse of that Heaven in 2 Corinthians 12, which he described as "seeing things of which it is not lawful to speak." He saw it! He knew it was "better by far" than the best experience of this life. And he couldn't wait to go.

All the glories, all the bliss, all the perfection of Heaven as it now exists are summarized in that one phrase, to "be with Christ, which is better by far." Heaven is with Jesus. In Jesus. Never separated again from Him. Ever in His presence. If your desire or image of Heaven can be fulfilled without Jesus in the picture, you have a distorted and un-biblical view of it.

Some people might say, "Well I don't want to go to Heaven and be stuck in church service all day. That's just tedious and boring." Let me allow Francis Chan to continue:

Can you imagine being in that setting and feeling bored? Feeling like you needed something more? Wishing people were being more attentive to your needs? There's no way! This is what we were made for! We're not doing people any favors by pretending they are the center of the universe. Either people will be awed by the sacred or they will not. If the sacred is not enough, then it is clear that the Spirit has not yet done a work in their lives.

Those who have gone before us to the throne of God have stood in awe for as long as they have been in the Presence of God. It has never grown old. I can't image it could be any other way. It has never gotten boring. Never been tiring. I don't think worship ever ceases in Heaven, but it takes a form unlike our worship "services" on earth, which pale in comparison. And boring is not on the menu! They are continually being "awed by the sacred!"

Then I saw in the right hand of him who was seated on the throne a scroll, written within and on the back, sealed with seven seals. And I saw a mighty angel proclaiming with a loud voice, "Who is worthy to open the scroll and break its seals?" And no one in heaven or on earth or under the earth was able to open the scroll or to look into it, and I began to weep loudly because no one was found worthy to open the scroll or to look into it. And one of the elders said to me, "Weep no more; behold, the Lion of the tribe of Judah, the Root of David, has conquered, so that he can open the scroll and its seven seals."

And between the throne and the four living creatures and among the elders I saw a Lamb standing, as though it had been slain,

*with seven horns and with seven eyes, which are the seven spirits of
God sent out into all the earth. And he went and took the scroll from
the right hand of him who was seated on the throne. And when he had
taken the scroll, the four living creatures and the twenty-four elders
fell down before the Lamb, each holding a harp, and golden bowls full
of incense, which are the prayers of the saints. And they sang a new
song, saying,*

*"Worthy are you to take the scroll
and to open its seals,
for you were slain, and by your blood you ransomed people for God
from every tribe and language and people and nation,
and you have made them a kingdom and priests to our God,
and they shall reign on the earth."*

*Then I looked, and I heard around the throne and the living creatures
and the elders the voice of many angels, numbering myriads of myriads and thousands of thousands, saying with a loud voice,*

*"Worthy is the Lamb who was slain,
to receive power and wealth and wisdom and might
and honor and glory and blessing!"*

*And I heard every creature in heaven and on earth and under the
earth and in the sea, and all that is in them, saying,*

*"To him who sits on the throne and to the Lamb
be blessing and honor and glory and might forever and ever!"
And the four living creatures said, "Amen!" and the elders fell down
and worshiped.*

—Revelation 5

Worship in Heaven will fully engage all of our personhood: mind, body, and spirit. Fully. It will renew us, energize us, and feed us. While worship happens around the throne, God is also giving instructions and sending angels out to do His bidding. Redemption continues to be accomplished. World history is being worked out, and those in the throne room around the Lamb see it, and interact with it.

What will we be doing? Well, from the time between our arrival there and our return to earth with Jesus at His triumphant inauguration, we will gaze into our Savior's face as we are finally, fully made like Him. The day of assignments for His saints is coming when they return as part of His glorious army of the redeemed. And those already in Heaven are being continually prepared for that great day of His return, and of their return to earth with Him.

My son-in-law and daughter have recently come to Florida to pastor a congregation near me. They have been in another state for over five years serving a church there. But a few years ago, their hearts began longing to return to Florida.

As they have prayed and waited for a door of opportunity to open, Patrick downloaded a picture of the skyline of Jacksonville, Florida on his iPhone. He kept it to remind himself of the dream God had put in his heart, and when times grew discouraging for him or my daughter Allison, he would pull the picture up on his phone and say, "One day God is going to call us back to Jacksonville."

A few months ago, that statement of faith became sight. They came to Jacksonville. For Christmas, my daughter purchased a framed picture of the skyline of Jacksonville to remind them of God's faithfulness in keeping His promise to them!

They couldn't wait to get "home." I wonder if you have a picture of "home" hanging in your heart? That wonderful place God is one day going to lead all of His saints to occupy?

And when we really understand how incredibly amazing it is, ...why wouldn't we want to go?

"Surrounded by His glory what will my heart feel;
Will I dance for you, Jesus, or in awe of You be still?
Will I sing Hallelujah or to my knees will I fall
Will I be able to speak at all
I can only imagine, I can only imagine."

—I Can Only Imagine
Mercy Me

CHAPTER 17:

BEYOND THE BAD NEWS TO THE GOOD NEWS

Joseph Stowell relates the story of a family who attended his church in Milwaukee, Wisconsin. The Willis' were an ordinary family focused on raising their children for the Lord. Duane "Scott" Willis was a schoolteacher and served occasionally in part-time ministry. His wife Janet spent her days homeschooling their six children still at home, ranging from three weeks of age to thirteen years.

Their three older children (nine kids in total) had moved out to begin families of their own. One fateful day the Willis family piled into the family van for a road trip to visit one of the elder siblings. Driving along the interstate, the unthinkable happened. A piece of metal dropped off a truck in front of them, went underneath their van and punctured the fuel tank.

The van immediately erupted into flames and Scott and Janet were both on fire when they jumped from the vehicle. As they looked back, the van was totally engulfed in flames, and five of their six children were entombed in the vehicle.

Janet could only manage to scream over and over to no one and to everyone, "No!" "No!" "No!" Scott tried to comfort his wife in her agony even as he was experiencing the same. All five children died in the fire, and the sixth who had gotten out of the vehicle died at the hospital the next morning.

The newspapers and networks picked up the tragic story, and Scott and Janet requested a news conference a couple of days after the accident. The Chicago Tribune article bore witness to their grace and incredible courage during the conference. Scott said in the conference, called for the purpose of bearing witness to their unwavering belief that sustained them, "God has purposes and God has reasons. He has shown incredible love to our family, and there is no question in our mind that God is always good."

Later Scott revealed what he had privately said to Janet to comfort her as they stood watching the burning van on the highway. He told her, "Janet this is what we have prepared ourselves and our children for...their death was quick...they are with the Lord. They are in heaven with the Lord."

A World Aflame with Sin

You do not have to search far to come to the conclusion that something in our world is badly broken. We need look no further than the story of the Willis family: godly, humble, loving God and loving each other, to see something is terribly wrong in this world. It is broken beyond the repair offered by better political legislation or leadership; beyond a more thorough-going education; beyond acquiring more money; beyond offering benevolent assistance to the poor in Third World countries; beyond better and more accessible medical care; even beyond ending hunger or poverty or the abuse and sexual trafficking of children as much as these must be ended.

It is broken in fundamental and foundational ways by sin. It is not just our personal and individual sins I am talking about. The brokenness and darkness permeates the very world system and emanates in chaos, violence, strife, war, murder, and death. It impacts good people and evil people; religious and irreligious alike. All are affected...none are excluded. And the reason is the outflowing of sin that visited the human race from the fall of Adam onward.

The whole creation groans...we live in a groaning, broken world. The pain is like that experienced by a woman giving birth. It is getting worse and worse and the outcome of the groaning coming closer together. Something is ready to break. Something has to give. The environment and the very foundation of the world we live in is steeped in this sin.

God did not create hurricanes and cancer, drought and starvation, war and hatred. He did not turn His "good" creation into a "groaning" creation. Our adversary, the devil, has torn apart what the Father created and he has re-created this world in his own image. His responsibility and rebellion that resulted in the fall of man has set the course of this planet and indeed, the very universe itself onto a collision course with the wrath of God. Something radical must happen to end the suffering and chaos. Sin and its results must be once-for-all eradicated. Doing so will come at a very high price.

The Price of Renewal

The price of our sin debt was paid in full by Jesus on the cross. Jesus went to the cross for the purpose of reconciling God and man, and that meant a price had to be paid for the offenses leveled against a holy God. God could not be just if He forgave without this price being paid. He could not be holy if He allowed His holiness to be affronted without consequence.

But God was also loving. He did not want to destroy the human race which had been made in His image. And so He made a way by offering His only begotten Son as a mediator between God and man; a lamb to be slain for the sins of the world; a sacrifice for the sins of the people.

And those who hear the truth of the Gospel and do not reject it will be among those whose sins can be forgiven completely, "by grace through faith." Our faith in the sacrifice of Jesus on the cross for us is all that is necessary for God's grace to flood our lives with His forgiveness and mercy.

A Christian is a person who, by that saving faith and amazing grace, find they are no longer "children of wrath" but are now children of the King, being transferred from the Kingdom of darkness to the kingdom of His Son.

The Rest of the Story

But it is more than our personal salvation that is at stake in God's redemptive agenda. While being rescued from "the wrath to come" is certainly an important facet, it does not complete God's plan. His plan is to redeem and make everything new! The entire universe is affected by Adam's sin. Nothing escapes it's impact.

A wealthy man began an adulterous affair with a woman in his company and this resulted in his faithful wife of over 25 years being evicted from their lovely and opulent home. In a matter of weeks, she went from loving wife and the center of the social circle to a person without a home. All due to her husband's infidelity.

As she was packing her belongings to move, she devised a plan. She secured a couple of pounds of fresh shrimp and stuffed them in the hollow curtain rods in every room in the house. Then she moved out.

In a matter of just a few days an odor became obvious, and then, over the next weeks...intolerable. The man hired cleaning firms and used scented products to cover the smell but to no avail. No one seemed able to locate the source of this horrific smell. And so, in desperation, they decided to sell the house and move elsewhere. He sold it for nearly one hundred thousand dollars below market value, just to get rid of it!

But as the house was being prepared for their move, the woman (who refused to live in the house) texted her new boyfriend and reminded him: "Tell the moving company to be sure and take the curtain rods."

Sin stains everything. It leaves an aroma of death wherever it visits, and it is an odor that can't be eliminated and one that we cannot escape. This world we live in, with all it's beauty and splendor, is a home that is sin-polluted. And no matter where we go, it goes with us in this fallen world. The only answer is to completely eliminate everything contaminated by sin's stain.

The Apocalypse of Peter

As we come now to a consideration of Peter's second letter, it should probably be said that this is the most "unfamiliar" of Peter's contributions to the New Testament. Mark's Gospel is actually Peter's eyewitness account related to and written down by his sister's son, John Mark.

And most people with a passing acquaintance of the New Testament will recognize 1 Peter. But the three chapters that make up this brief New Testament correspondence pack a wallop! Sometimes referred to as "The Apocalypse of Peter" these chapters and particularly Chapter 3 outline a dire conclusion to our universe and our planet.

Peter and the Heretics

The third chapter of Peter is actually a work of apologetic genius. Peter is defending the faith against false teachers and heretical views that had begun taking root in the early churches. First the skeptics and heretics scoffed and mocked the believers by saying, "Where is this promise of His coming?" In other words, "God has waited so long to send Christ back why should we believe He's going to do it?"

This is now, beloved, the second letter I am writing to you in which I am stirring up your sincere mind by way of reminder, that you should remember the words spoken beforehand by the holy prophets and the commandment of the Lord and Savior spoken by your apostles. Know this first of all, that in the last days mockers will come with their mocking, following after their own lusts, and saying, "Where is the promise of His coming? For ever since the fathers fell asleep, all continues just as it was from the beginning of creation. (2 Peter 3:1-4 NASB)

This particular viewpoint also argued for the continuity of creation, meaning that God is not going to let anything interrupt the world He has created. To this Peter responded:

For when they maintain this, it escapes their notice that by the word of God the heavens existed long ago and the earth was formed out of water and by water, through which the world at that time was destroyed, being flooded with water. But by His word the present heavens and earth are being reserved for fire, kept for the day of judgment and destruction of ungodly men. (2 Peter 3:5-7 NASB)

Peter reminds them of two incredible events of God's interruption. First, he reminds them of God's creative activity in first creating the heavens and then, out of the chaos of the water, created and formed our planet. Further, Peter reminds them of the worldwide flood in Noah's day described in Genesis. It was truly a cataclysmic worldwide event. Even the word "cataclysm" ("overflowed") is a reference to what God did in judging the earth with water in the Book of Genesis.

Both are indications that God has and will again interrupt His creation to accomplish judgment. The promise of God made to Noah and to all of humanity was that the earth would never again be destroyed by a cataclysmic flood. That promise is secure. However, another vehicle of judgment is "waiting in reserve" for those who will not repent and return to the Lord.

But do not let this one fact escape your notice, beloved, that with the Lord one day is like a thousand years, and a thousand years like one day. The Lord is not slow about His promise, as some count slowness, but is patient toward you, not wishing for any to perish but for all to come to repentance. But the day of the Lord will come like a thief, in which the heavens will pass away with a roar and the elements will be destroyed with intense heat, and the earth and its works will be burned up. (2 Peter 3:8-10 NASB)

Peter now turns, in verse 8, to defending the speed with which God has chosen to bring judgment to the earth. His argument has to do with the nature of time from God's viewpoint and ours. "...one day is like a thousand years, and a thousand years like one day."

But God's apparent slowness in keeping His promise of bringing judgment is not God Second guessing His decision or being lax, but in reality is God's mercy toward those yet to repent.

The Final Cataclysm

The final judgment God will bring to the planet earth will not be an overflowing of water in a flood, but an overflowing of fire that will burn "the heavens" and everything in them. This image is not the first time it has occurred in the Bible. Isaiah has a similar prophecy about the stars falling from the sky as the heavens are rolled up like a scroll.

This is not, as some have imagined, a final great nuclear war that destroys the planet. This is, in every sense of the language, something God will do Himself. Directly. No other hand but His in this final conflagration of fire in which "the elements will be burn up with intense heat." Everything will be reduced to the state with which God began at creation. Every star, planet, galaxy, asteroid...everything will be purified in this intense heat that will melt it all.

But What About Heaven?

"But wait a minute," you might ask. "I thought this was about heaven?" Oh, it is. But to completely understand what Heaven is, we need to more fully understand what God's plan is for the earth!

You see from the beginning, it was God's desire to create a sanctuary. A place where He could meet and dwell with and fellowship with His creation. You. Me. The earth, the universe, and all that was in it were intended to be that sanctuary.

The epicenter of it all was the Garden of Eden; an unparalleled sanctuary. God "walked with Adam in the cool of the day." He tabernacled; "camped out" with His creation which was His delight.

But sin destroyed that tabernacle, and it was necessary for Him to banish Adam and Eve from this sanctuary where sin had no place or part. And from that time forward, God sought a way for this sanctuary to be recreated and re-established on earth with His creation.

It has never been God's intention to eliminate this planet we now live on, and allow us to live in "hover board Heaven" floating above it all. Revelation ends with the stirring affirmation, as the New Jerusalem descends, that "the dwelling of God is now with man!"

We are not going to live in some ethereal, cloud-based floating sky city. Heaven, as the Bible describes it, is right here on the earth you are now living on. You see, we've gotten something badly confused in our thinking and teaching about our Father's intent.

As desperate as we are to get off the planet, God is desperate to get on it! This world, this globe we live on is not disposable goods. It will one day be made eternally durable, just as your earthly body will be. All sins will have been purified and burned away by God's final judgment of this world.

And His ultimate plan is to plant the Heavenly City, the New Jerusalem, squarely in the place where the Garden of Eden was first located. He will compete what He started at creation. Sin will not be victorious in derailing His ultimate plan to redeem the heavens and earth. The curse of sin will once for all be lifted.

Martin Lloyd-Jones offered this:

Everything will be glorified, even nature itself. And that seems to be the biblical teaching about the eternal state: that what we call heaven is life in this perfect world as God intended humanity to live it. When he put Adam in the Paradise at the beginning, Adam fell and all fell with him, but men and women are meant to live in the body, and will live in a glorified body in a glorified world, and God will be with them.

—*Great Doctrines of the Bible*

In that incredible, perfect and eternal dwelling place, "the lion will lie down with the lamb, and they will not seek to hurt or make war anymore." The things that require justice will be made right. The unrighteous will be made holy. The effects of sin will be erased. Creation will no longer groan. The stench of sin and death will be replaced by the fragrance of Christ's Presence with us. The dwelling of God will be with man. "And he will wipe away all tears from their eyes for the former things have passed away."

And in that day, the Heavens and the earth will rejoice!

CHAPTER 18:

BEYOND THE VALLEY TO THE ETERNAL CITY

"Aim at heaven, and you get earth thrown in.
Aim at earth, and you get neither."
—CS Lewis

As I began an earlier section on eternity, I suggested that many have a view of heaven that is inadequate. It is a mixture of biblical truth, superstition, understandings from other cultures, bad hymns, and cartoons. Much of what we hear and have been conditioned to think about our eternal destiny, even in church, is much more folksy than biblical. Certainly, as we look at this culturally-created view of heaven, we do not have an image in mind that is better than the happiness we feel we can achieve in this life. And we do not have something we would give our lives joyfully to receive as early Christians were more than willing to do to obtain it.

It is not a definition that has substance, and no matter how pretty or sentimentalized we can make it, it will not bear the weight of giving hope in a life of suffering and hardship. We suspect deep within that our view of God's promised eternity for us, our "inheritance that cannot be defiled," has distorted by this view and contains much that is simply not true.

One place where we are most lacking in biblical truth and understanding is the exact form and shape and even the whereabouts of our eternal home. Is it circling around "out there" on a cloud outside the reach of the Hubble telescope and satellites and massive radar dishes?

Is it on another planet, as some religions have surmised? Does it exist in another undetectable dimension, as some who are more scientifically-minded seem to suggest? Does it even exist in our reality at all, or is it just religious idealism? Is it, as physicists at Yale, and Harvard and other elite schools are now surmising with string theory, a reality that exists in another of ten dimensions (or more) of reality? Obviously there is much we do not know.

But we can answer some of these questions with biblical certainty:

The Heavenly city is a place. Jesus called it that in John 14:1-3 when He said, "I am going to prepare a place for you." There is a specific location to our Heavenly home.

The Heavenly city is built by God. This city which the earliest of the faithful sought is a city whose "builder and maker is God." It's foundation has been laid by our Father Himself.

The Heavenly city is outside the scope of our universe. It is a city that cannot be tainted or stained by sin, and all sin is forever locked outside it's doors. Therefore it could not exist in the physical universe that we live in since sin has affected everything we can see with our eyes, no matter how far we manage to travel to galaxies far away.

The Heavenly city is a place of ceaseless joy and celebration. Hebrews 12:22-24 tells us:

But you have come to Mount Zion, to the city of the living God, the heavenly Jerusalem. You have come to thousands upon thousands of angels in joyful assembly, to the church of the firstborn, whose names are written in heaven. You have come to God, the Judge of all, to the spirits of the righteous made perfect, to Jesus the mediator of a new covenant, and to the sprinkled blood that speaks a better word than the blood of Abel.

From just a brief description, we can conclude that "heaven" is a concrete, tangible place; it will be a physical place, with literal dimensions and scale and scope, and not just vapor and clouds; it is a joyful place; it is a place built personally by the hand of God; it is a place occupied by our Savior and it is not within our ability to see it with human eyes...at least not yet. It is mysterious, and yet the closing words of the Bible occupy themselves with giving us a picture of the home where Jesus longs to bring His Bride to live.

The descriptive list we could compile goes on. But nowhere do we get a clearer glimpse of what is awaiting the redeemed in eternity than in Revelation 21-22. The book that "unveils" and "reveals" eternal truths long hidden will one day pour forth its secrets now hard to understand.

We get a foretaste; a glimpse of what is coming in these concluding chapters: after the apocalypse and calamity and judgement of the universe by fire; after sin is banished forever; after the enemy has been imprisoned for all eternity in his rightful home. So what does this eternal dwelling hold for us?

A Portrait of Heaven

If you have sought to sell a home in the past decade or two, you have probably done so being greatly helped by the internet. There you have the opportunity to post photos of your home, your yard, your neighborhood. A curious shopper or serious buyer relies heavily on these photos for initial impressions, but they can also be decisive in closing a real estate deal.

We like pictures. We can grasp the images and tie our imaginations easily to photographs and internet postings. And so it is fitting that God has chosen to lead His chosen and inspired writer, John, to conclude not only the Book of Revelation but the entire Bible with an elaborate portrait of the place prepared for us to live in eternally.

A Heavenly City

In the last chapter, we dealt with the coming day when the judgement of God comes to completely cleanse and purify our existing world and universe. Revelation 21 begins with that picture:

Then I saw a new heavens and a new earth, for the first heaven and the first earth had passed away, and there was no longer any sea.
(Revelation 21:1)

The Bible begins with the affirmation and narrative of God's creation of the heavens and the earth. It is fitting that it ends with God's renewal of the heavens and earth. But it is the same one that has been recreated, not a different one that is made. God did not start "ex nihlio," or out of nothing. He began with a purified earth and universe. Much of the shape and form of the new heavens and new earth will have a familiar look to us.

Some believe that when God starts again, He will revert everything back to the Garden of Eden. We will be like innocents roaming the Garden, there to begin our exploration, our progress, our technology, our advances as the human race all over again.

But the heaven that's described in these chapters is nothing of the sort. It will be a place of architectural and artistic marvels, of buildings and structures, of roadways (yes, paved with gold!), of a glorious light in the center of it all which means that no sun and no energy source was ever needed "for the glory of the Lord was it's light."

168

(Revelation 21:23)

In this new heaven and new earth, God will dwell with man. That was His intent from the very beginning. The believer in Christ would not want a Heaven without God present with them. God is present, but death, and mourning, and crying and pain will have no place, for "God will wipe away all tears from their eyes." (Revelation 21:4). He is going to "make all things new!" (Revelation 21:5)

But also in this imagery is something we often miss. John identified the "Holy City, the new Jerusalem," coming down out of heaven as a bride "beautifully dressed for her husband." (Revelation 21:2). We find ourselves challenged here by the imagery of the city.

Our belief has long been, at least as long as I can remember, that we were going to be living in "mansions just over the hilltop," walking on "streets paved with gold" and hoping that we get a house next door to Jesus! But here we learn that we, the bride, *are* the city! The city is the Bride. The Church is the Bride. Therefore the city is the Bride.

Now while that may not make sense to us literally, it is a picture of the adornment and glory that God is going to pour out on His beloved in that day. The city will descend from heaven (as John saw this) like a bride coming down the stairs for a beautiful wedding feast! It is a wonderful picture of the glory that God will cloth His people with in that day.

The remainder of Revelation 21 describes with great detail and measurements the city that is descending. It is described in measurement as a cube, fifteen hundred meters in length, depth, and height, which is architecturally difficult to image.

However, were it to be seen literally we are talking about a city that would stretch from Canada to Mexico and from the Appalachian Mountains to California. And again, it is as high as it is long and wide. It would be massive in square footage and, let's remember, the Bible mentions fifteen times in Revelation 21 and 22 that it is a "city." In addition to these measurements of the dimension of the city, the jewels and metals used are also listed as building materials (Revelation 21:10-21).

Symbolism in Revelation is so important. We tear up some of the most important spiritual images by trying to force them into a literal description. The "cube" in biblical times was a description of something that was in every way geometrically perfect. It would have reminded at least the Jewish readers of the description of the Holy of Holies of Solomon's temple where God came down and met with the priests. The dimensions of this city are perfectly proportioned and according to translator Bruce Metzger, "absolutely splendid, with a harmony and symmetry of perfect proportions." In this instance, the entire city would become the Holy of Holies! This seems to me a more important dimension of the text even than the architectural details.

A Heavenly Light

It might be expected that in the center of this scene of a magnificent city that a worship center or tabernacle or temple would exist. But the Bible is clear that no such location exists, because "the Lord God Almighty and the Lamb are the temple." (Revelation 21:22)

Something that would be akin to the "shekinah glory" of God provides the illumination of the city. It will provide light for all who come to it to bring "honor and glory" into it. (Revelation 21:24). And the gates will not be shut at all for there is no night there!

Imagine. There is no need for a security system. No darkness is there for a thief or mugger to hide. There is light emanating from every crack and crevice of the city. And nothing defiling will enter the city, but access will be allowed only those "written in the Lamb's book of life." (Revelation 21:27)

A Heavenly Garden

In Revelation 22, the imagery moves away from a description of the city of the Bride to the city of the Garden. It begins with a description of "the river of the water of life, as clear as crystal, flowing from the throne of God and of the Lamb down the middle of the great street of the city." Straddled across the river on both sides is the "tree of life, bearing twelve crops of fruit and yielding it's fruit every month." The leaves of the tree are for "the healing of the nations."

Clearly what we are reading is a return of those things forfeited because of man's fall in the Garden. Commentator Philip Hughes tells us that "The river with its water of life symbolizes the inexhaustible grace of God."

I love rivers. I currently live in a city with seven bridges. Jacksonville, Florida is a city on the St Johns River, one of only two rivers that flow south to north in the world! I grew up in Ashland,Kentucky on the banks of the Ohio River, and moved to Louisville and lived there also on the Ohio River. I have never lived anywhere without a river near by.

So I am thrilled to hear our heavenly home will be built with a river flowing right down the middle of it, bringing replenishing, refreshing everlasting water to all who would come and drink. How different from the dark, polluted waterways of this world. These are rivers of life-giving eternal water, that living water Jesus taught the Samaritan woman about in John 4.

Not only are the waters replenishing and grace-filled and abundant, but the tree of life in the center of it all will provide it's fruit abundantly, with twelve different kinds of fruit provided each month. What incredible grace for our Creator to give us that which we had once forfeited through sin!

But the curse will be gone. "There will be no more curse..." (Revelation 22:3), but "the throne of God and of the Lamb" will be in its midst and his servants will serve him eternally. Greatest of all, "they will see His face..." We will know our God face-to-face, and not be destroyed! Even more than that, we will be known by Him: "His name will be on their foreheads."

How different from the fate of those who received the mark of the beast earlier in the Book of Revelation. As they did so, and chose to follow the Beast, they forfeited the opportunity to know God and to be known personally by Him. What a tragic sacrifice will be made when that takes place!

Finally "there will be no night there" for the Lord God gives them light and they will reign forever and ever." (Revelation 22:5). Light will characterize and constantly bathe this massive, eternal and incredible city of God!

The Real Heaven

So with this portrait of our heavenly home hanging before us, we need to understand some things more deeply than we often take time to think about. Once again, much of our thinking about eternity is not grounded in reality, but more often in sentimentality.

I am not arguing against people wanting to see loved ones in heaven who have gone before. There is nothing wrong with such a desire. I believe my own wife's experience on her death bed indicates that there is some "connection" between the believers who have died and a loved one nearing death. I would do nothing to take that comfort from anyone. I myself look forward to seeing her and my beloved family already at home there!

However, I must at the same time emphasize that the ultimate joy of heaven for the believer is the joy of being in the presence of the Lord in unbroken fellowship forever. That is where our true joy and encouragement come. At the end of it all, heaven is being with Jesus. Period.

An Intermediate Heaven?

It quickly becomes difficult to try to assemble a timeline of when heaven as we see it in Revelation 21-22 will come to pass. I will leave it to more skilled interpreters than myself to identify and analyze those issues. Many ideas have been set forth to explain it.

However, it is very apparent that what we are viewing in Revelation 21-22 is, first of all, not the place we as believers go immediately. This is an end time celebration and is described, in fact, much like a wedding celebration. The Bride is not yet gathered completely in heaven yet and therefore the wedding cannot take place.

It does provide us with an understanding of what will ultimately be our destiny as children of the Heavenly Father. But in the mean-time...what? Is there something else that happens? Where do my loved ones go when they go to sleep in Christ...where will I go?

The simplest answer, and it's not simple, is that we will go to be with Christ. Where ever He is, there the child of God will be. Some have called this an "intermediate state," or an "intermediate heaven." A tem-porary one. It is a place the Bible assures us is "paradise."

But it is a place where those who have already gone to be with Jesus have gone, fully alive, fully awake, fully conscious and without pain or any suffering. But it is an incomplete state. They have not yet received the fullness of their resurrection experience by receiving a glo-rified body that is part of redemption's promise to us.

Unlike the view of many of the world's religions, Christianity is a very physically-focused belief system. It does not see the body as something to be shed like a locust's shell or to be fled like a prison cell. The body does not "trap" us and hold us down. It is us! We are not com-partmentalized creatures that can be segmented into pieces. God re-deems the whole, and that includes the final glorification of the body.

As we noted earlier, it will be a place of unending adoration and worship of the Lamb of God, the lamb who was worthy and who was slain. The saints who have gone already into God's presence gather there in worship and adoration, standing in awe of the Lamb. We know that the experience of worship in Revelation 4 and 5 is before the final descent of the Heavenly city because the martyrs are seen still crying out for God to bring vengeance for their suffering.

It is worship in an intermediate state of eternity that will be folded into the final pages of Revelation when Jesus returns with His saints now with Him. (1 Thessalonians 4:13-16) We are not told much of what it will look like, but we do have the picture of our final state in the New Jerusalem that will come down out of Heaven. And we know these two things: First, we will see Jesus. And second, we will never see death. For those who name Jesus as Savior, those two things will be enough. None could ever ask for a more glorious reward and reality or a more gratifying and satisfying eternity. John Donne wrote,

I shall rise from the dead...I shall see the Son of God, the Son of Glory, and shine myself as that sun shines. I shall be united to the Ancient of Days, to God Himself, who had no morning, never began...No man ever saw God and lived. And yet, I shall not live until I see God; and when I have seen Him I shall never die.

"And I will dwell in the house of the Lord forever." (Psalm 23:6)

CHAPTER 19:

BEYOND ANXIETY TO JOY

Rejoice in the Lord always. Again I will say, rejoice! Let your gentleness be known to all men. The Lord is at hand. Be anxious for nothing, but in everything by prayer and supplication, with thanksgiving, let your requests be made known to God; and the peace of God, which surpasses all understanding, will guard your hearts and minds through Christ Jesus. Finally, brethren, whatever things are true, whatever things are noble, whatever things are just, whatever things are pure, whatever things are lovely, whatever things are of good report, if there is any virtue and if there is anything praiseworthy—meditate on these things. The things which you learned and received and heard and saw in me, these do, and the God of peace will be with you.

(Philippians 4:6-9)

An Indian guru named Mehar Baba made a decision never to talk. He actually never spoke for 40 years. Baba believed he was "the avatar of the age," and was God in the flesh.

He wrote with an alphabet board when he wanted to communicate his teaching. He believed the universe was just the imagination of a divine being, and none of it is real, therefore there's nothing for us to worry about. His most famous saying? You already know it: "Don't worry, be happy."

One of his most famous students was singer Bobby McFerrin. McFerrin took his teaching and popularized it in a song..and the catchy little ditty entitled "Don't Worry, Be Happy" became the first acapella Billboard hit.

But is that all there is to getting beyond anxiety? Humming a happy little tune and convincing yourself that the world around you isn't real and doesn't really matter anyway?

The number one health threat in America for women is anxiety. For men, it's drug and alcohol abuse which is often an issue because of anxiety as well. We are an anxiety-prone culture. The use of anti-psychotic and anti-anxiety medications are at an all-time high in our nation today. In a seven year period Americans more than doubled purchases of medications like Xanax and Valium, jumping from $900 million to $2.1 billion. In seven years! Millions more are being spent annually on research.

And it's affecting our kids big time. Dr Robert Leahy suggests that the average child today has as many anxiety issues as the average psychiatric patient had in the 1950's. What's causing this? Rapid change. Overuse of technology and information overload....a crisis in Nepal is made to feel as close as if it happened thirty miles away. There is no longer the buffer zone of informational flow that used to be in place. The world doesn't seem to be a safe place; many of our children have never known anything but a post 9/11 world and a shaky economy and school shootings. Everything's a crisis. Everything in their world creates anxiety.

Now, I understand that some people face a deep-rooted anxiety that has been a part of their brain chemistry since birth. Others have experienced deep trauma or PTSD. According to one study, about thirty percent of our anxiety- related problems are genetic, part of our DNA, or hereditary. Those people will need medication and professional therapy to cope. But that means seventy percent of it is conditioned and learned which means it can also be unlearned.

Neurobiology teaches us that the neural channels that carry information from our brains to our eyes actually send more information from the brain to the eyes than the eyes send to the brain. Your brain conditions what you see, and how you interpret it. Our thoughts actually become a part of our physical makeup over time. Every thought we have is mirrored in our bodies. Your body changes to keep up with the thoughts that come it's way.

We condition ourselves to perceive an event, a word, a story as a threat—provoking anxiety through the information coming from our brain to our optic nerves, and then our emotions respond to the information whether it is objectively true or not. We literally can...and often do...reinforce and program ourselves to be anxious!

But many of us are just derailed by garden-variety worry: anxious thoughts that keep us awake or keep waking us at night, or just being stuck in indecision and fear. Rick Warren said that worrying is like sitting in a rocking chair. A lot of activity takes place, but you go nowhere.

At it's core, anxiety is a response to a fear, real or imagined, that you are wrestling with. Jesus said, "Stop being anxious."

In Hawaii, they call mainlanders (the English speaking tribes) "haole." The word, as best we can translate Polynesian, is "breathless one." The name was used for early English settlers who came to the laid-back Polynesian islands and immediately started to build hospitals, schools, and orphanages. They were always out of breath, working at a frantic pace.

Now you may say, "Ok all of this may be true. But telling me to "stop being anxious" is not that simple. You can't just turn it off." Well Jesus seemed to think you can. He said it repeatedly. (Luke 12:22-31). And the Apostles picked up where Jesus left off. Fear is a learned response to a perceived threat. We can choose to be upbeat or beat up by life.

My granddaughter McCail is not afraid of dogs. My Dad was. He had learned to fear the dog's bark, growl, or even a dog jumping up on him to lick him. But he had to learn it. McCail hasn't yet learned to fear dogs, but I've seen dogs fear her!

Children are not by nature afraid of strangers. You have to teach them to be. We learn to fear things in the world around us: dogs or disease, or nuclear war or the economy failing or the stock market crashing or a terrorist or deranged person invading our kids school. Bad things do happen. People get shot in church. Christians get sick...get cancer...and die. Anxiety is the big "WHAT IF" we hang over those possibilities that shuts our lives down under an avalanche of fear.

If I could present you today with a pill...a medication....that would end anxiety for you once and for all, would you be eager to take it? Most would. (Again, many spend big money every year doing that). And yet Jesus has spoken words that give freedom from anxiety but we don't want to hear them. If we would just take the Word of God at face value and do what it says, within three weeks to a month much of your anxiety would be gone. At the same time, let me set the record straight. We're going to worry about some things.

We live in a world where worry is a reasonable response to all the millions of threats....terrorist attacks, diseases, weather disasters, even global warming.

But there's a difference in fear and anxiety. You may fear seeing a snake in your yard. I live in Florida. It's reasonable to be afraid and assume it might be a moccasin or other poisonous snake. Fear actually can save your life! Anxiety is saying, "There might be a poisonous snake in my yard, so I'm never going outside again." Now we are afraid of things that might be true, but we don't know if they are or not!

Last spring I went into my garden shed to retrieve a tool and there, hanging from the rafter was a four or five foot long snake skin. Somewhere the snake that left that behind may be lurking. It may be a ten foot long poisonous snake, maybe a boa constrictor or some collector's escaped cobra.

So I've decided to burn it down and build a new shed! Not really, but the reasonable assessment is this was a harmless (though VERY LONG) rat snake that is only a threat if you are a baby rat or baby squirrel. Since I am neither, I have nothing rationally to fear from the snake.

Fear is going to come our way. Worry is fear out of control. Again, some degree of fear is healthy. It keeps you from danger. But anxiety is the "what if" that can keep us imprisoned.

It is never healthy because it is not based in reality, but a fantasy we create that might possibly happen sometime in the future.

The Bureau of Statistics in Washington DC tells us that a fog that can shut down a city block, snarl traffic and make it difficult even to see ten feet in front of you consists of about two tablespoons of water! Worry is a fog that has very little substance to it.

The Apostle Paul penned the words of our text in the Book of Philippians, about 62 AD. In 55 AD, he wrote the letter called 2 Corinthians. In 2 Corinthians 11:28, Paul admitted to worrying...he speaks of "my anxiety for all the churches." Seven years later, we read about his personal coping mechanism in the Letter to the Philippians.

The Bible is Kindle's most highlighted book...and Philippians 4:4-6 is the most highlighted passage! I wonder if Paul knew this counsel would get that kind of publicity? Many of us cling to the hope of these words.

Basically Philippians 4:4-9 outlines four things we have to do to get control of anxiety.

These are not "generic" in the sense that just everybody or anybody can make it work. It is written for Christians to apply...which means that just because you're a Christian is no guarantee against worry and anxiety.

Four thoughts form the rungs of the ladder that provides us the way out of this pit. We must "rejoice in the Lord." We have to recalibrate how we find contentment, satisfaction, and even how we define happiness, and it begins here: We are to "rejoice in the Lord." (Philippians 4:9)

The First Rung

The first rung of our rescue ladder is this: Rejoice. This is why I say again that this formula for anxiety will work for you...if you are a believer. Who is a believer? A person who can "rejoice in the Lord."

These inspired words come as a command. Just as the command "don't be anxious" or "be anxious for nothing" is a command. The command literally says, "don't let anything perpetually and continually make you anxious." It doesn't say every time you're anxious you're disobedient. It says if you allow yourself to continually be trapped in the cycle of anxiety that is within your power to change, you are in disobedience.

In the same way in this passage of the Bible, Paul is saying, "Continually and perpetually rejoice in the Lord." That doesn't mean you're always going to be happy...you're not. Your circumstances may be difficult. I get phone calls or emails or text messages daily from people who are in tough circumstances right now. But their circumstances do not exempt them from this command.

Paul was writing from a prison cell...not a Caribbean beach house or the deck of a cruise ship. It may be understood that what he is advocating is rejoicing in spite of our circumstances. Do not wait until the diagnosis is known. Rejoice in the Lord now. Do not wait until your errant child comes back to restore your family to wholeness. Rejoice in the Lord now. Do not wait until the job offer is known, or your husband or wife agree to go for counseling. Rejoice in the Lord now. Rejoicing in the Lord is an attitude...a choice...a conscious decision we make to trust God's handling and outcome of our circumstance. He's got this. Trust Him for it.

Now let's be clear here. Paul is not advocating some form of "Don't worry, be happy" theology. He is saying this: If you are trying to find your cause for rejoicing in anything on this earth more than in the Lord, you have reason to be anxious. You could lose it. Your joy in your job? You can be downsized. Your joy in your car? You can scratch or wreck it. Your joy in your savings? Your health? You can lose them. Your ultimate joy in your family? They can be taken from you.

But if your ultimate joy is in the Lord, then your ultimate and greatest cause for rejoicing can never be taken from you! Over and over, this truth is expressed in Scripture:

1 Samuel 2: Hannah "My soul rejoices *in the Lord*"

Psalm 32:11: "Rejoice *in the Lord* and be glad, you his righteous."

Psalm 64:10: "Rejoice *in the Lord*, take refuge in Him and glory in His name."

Psalm 97:12: "Rejoice i*n the Lord*, you his righteous, and praise his holy name."

Psalm 104:35: ""May my meditation be pleasing to Him as I rejoice *in the Lord.*"

Isaiah 29:19: "Once more the humble will rejoice *in the Lord*...the needy will rejoice *in the Holy One of Israel*

Isaiah 41:16: "Rejoice i*n the Lord* and glory *in the Holy One of Israel.*"

Joel 2:23: "Be glad people of Zion and rejoice *in the Lord* your God, for He has given you the autumn rains because He is faithful."

Habakkuk 3:17-18. "Though the fig tree yield no harvest and there are no grapes on the vine, though the olive crops fail and there is no food , though there are no sheep in the pen or cattle in the stalls yet I will rejoice *in the Lord my God.*"

Zechariah 10:7 where the Lord promises that people will one day instinctively obey the command to rejoice i*n the Lord.*

I think this makes the point. Our joy is not found in pleasant circumstances, and it cannot be lost in bad ones. We rejoice "in the Lord"...He will not leave us nor be taken from us. There comes a time when you need to change your outlook to an uplook. WE can rejoice in God's presence, in His precepts, in His promises, in His provision, in His pardon, in His peace, in His providence.

We rejoice in the Lord. Many things we may look to in our life for happiness cannot really bring us lasting joy. Do you always rejoice in your job? Are you rejoicing today in your favorite sports team? Can your rejoice today in your marriage? How about rejoicing in your health? Rejoicing in your family? How about finding one day when you can rejoice in all of these...at the same time? Probably not going to happen.

But when you rejoice in the Lord there's never a time when you don't have something to rejoice in! Maybe the cause of so much anxiety in some of our lives simply lies here: We are trying to find joy in possessions and situations and even in people who ultimately can never bring it to us. Success, affluence, possessions, wealth, promotions, perfect families...perfect health. These things will all let you down at some point.

But God will not. Jesus never fails. The joy of the Lord can be your strength that carries you through days that could cause you anxiety. It's a joy that begins when you know Jesus Christ as your Savior by faith; your pardon through His blood and sacrifice for you on the cross. He died for your sin and guilt so you wouldn't have to! God's love was demonstrated through Jesus' death, and when you know that and surrender to that then you can know a joy that can never be taken from you...the joy of the Lord.

"Rejoice in the Lord always and again I say rejoice!"

The Second Rung

The second rung on the ladder is that we must intentionally, even ruthlessly release our anxiety. Some of us have a death grip on anxiety. We may think we have it under control, and yet, it is a poisonous serpent that is killing US! We just don't know how to let it go. Pastor and author Chuck Swindoll shares the following true story:

For years, I have kept close at hand a newspaper clipping about a man who fought a snake. He was hunting for deer in a remote wildlife area of Northern California when he climbed onto a ledge and whoomp!, a snake lunged at him, barely missing his neck. He instinctively grabbed the serpent several inches behind the head to keep from being bitten as the snake wrapped itself around his neck and shook its rattle furiously. When he tried to pull the reptile off, he discovered the fangs were caught in his wool turtleneck sweater...and he began to feel the venom dripping down the skin of his neck.He fell backward and slid headfirst down the steep slope through brush and lava rocks, his rifle and binoculars bouncing beside him. He ended up wedged between some rocks with his feet caught uphill from his head. Barely able to move, he got his right hand on his rifle and used it to disengage the fangs from his sweater, but the snake had enough leverage to strike again. The serpent lunged at him, over and over and over. He kept his face turned so the rattler couldn't get a good angle with its fangs, but he could feel the snake bumping its nose just below his eye. (From Living Beyond the Level of Mediocrity)

Fortunately the man in this story survived by strangling the deadly serpent to death. Likewise we must ruthlessly deal with anxiety or it will destroy us! There are no "ties" or compromises in this conflict. You win or you lose.

Jesus addressed this problem in the Gospel of Matthew:

Therefore I tell you, do not worry about your life, what you will eat or drink; or about your body, what you will wear. Is not life more than food, and the body more than clothes? Look at the birds of the air; they do not sow or reap or store away in barns, and yet your heavenly Father feeds them. Are you not much more valuable than they? Can any one of you by worrying add a single hour to your life?

"And why do you worry about clothes? See how the flowers of the field grow. They do not labor or spin. Yet I tell you that not even Solomon in all his splendor was dressed like one of these. If that is how God clothes the grass of the field, which is here today and tomorrow is thrown into the fire, will he not much more clothe you—you of little faith? So do not worry, saying, 'What shall we eat?' or 'What shall we drink?' or 'What shall we wear?' For the pagans run after all these things, and your heavenly Father knows that you need them. But seek first his kingdom and his righteousness, and all these things will be given to you as well. Therefore do not worry about tomorrow, for tomorrow will worry about itself. Each day has enough trouble of its own. (Matthew 6:25-32 ESV)

Jesus ends His teaching by assuring us of this one thing: God will provide the strength we need for anything that comes to us when we need it but not before. "Each day will have enough trouble of its own."

Like the Israelite's gathering manna in the wilderness, they could only collect and keep enough for one day, then they had to depend on and trust in the Lord to bring them their supply for the next day. This is a principle that follows God's dealing with people throughout the Bible: Give us this day our daily bread. It keeps our face turned toward God, and not our own strength to survive.

Anxiety spreads within us when we fast-forward into an uncertain and unknown future and try to play out different scenarios in our mind. The problem is, we can imagine whatever the worst case scenario might possibly be. But one important piece of the puzzle is left out: What is God going to bring to us in that moment to help us cope with that scenario?

Jesus promise to us is that God's "piece of the puzzle" will more than fit what we need in that moment. But we cannot peer into the future and see what that's going to be. We trust God today for what we need today, we seek His kingdom and righteousness first, and then we find...

He is always enough.

The Third Rung

The third rung of our ladder is this: We must make our requests known to God. God wants us to pray always! He wants us to *pray for everything....with thanksgiving.* "God I'm taking my child to the doctor today but I am making request to You to help the doctor find the right medicine or treatment." "God I have a meeting today with a prospective client...help me to have the right approach to gain their business." 'Lord, I am lonely and need a husband or wife. I am going on a date, but I'm asking You to lead me to know if this is a person You would want me to continue dating." "God I've got a test today...lots of stuff on it I'm not sure I understand."

Do you pray like that? Is your prayer life a vital, real, ongoing conversation with God or is it just a thoughtless "O by the way God would you bless this or that" like we would remind our spouse to pick up milk at the grocery? We are to "pray without ceasing." We are "in all things to give thanks and pray," and not just call on God when we're in a hard spot.

Recently I led a group of folks through an in-depth study of the Letters of John. 1 John ends with a chapter that summarizes our confidence and assurance before God because of our faith in Jesus Christ. 1 John 5:14-15 tells us that "whatever we ask according to His will He will do it."

Now this is the confidence that we have in Him, that if we ask anything according to His will, He hears us. And if we know that He hears us, whatever we ask, we know that we have the petitions that we have asked of Him. (1 John 5:14-15 NKJV)

That is, by all measures, an astounding promise and assurance. Whatever we ask! Whenever we ask something that is His will He will do it—every prayer we pray according to His will.

And while that promise is as sure as God's Word is true, what we are not told is *when* God will do it. Sometimes the answer is not given in the timeline we would prefer. It does not say that God will immediately perform what we ask. If that were true then God has just turned Himself into a cosmic trick pony, and turned His Sovereignty over to us! Yet He gives us the assurance that He does hear us when we pray, and when we pray according to His will, He does what we have prayed for. We must then wait in faith that it will be accomplished.

The Fourth Rung

The fourth and final rung on the is the need to *renew your thinking*. Let's go back to a fundamental place: Anxiety is a battle for our minds. It's about how we think, but also about what we think *about*. The thoughts we think form the emotions we have.

Romans 12:1-2 tells us we are not to be conformed to this world but instead to be "transformed by the renewing of our minds." Our transformation begins with changing the way we think about God, our identity in Him, and the world we live in.

Later in Philippians we read a detailed list of the things that should replace our anxious thoughts:

Finally, brothers, whatever is true, whatever is honorable, whatever is just, whatever is pure, whatever is lovely, whatever is commendable, if there is any excellence, if there is anything worthy of praise, think about these things. What you have learned and received and heard and seen in me—practice these things, and the God of peace will be with you. (Philippians 4:8-9 ESV)

Our thoughts sometimes make God much too small. We make God smaller than He really is. We convince ourselves that God isn't aware of our issues...or He isn't smart enough to fix them...not strong enough to handle them...not big enough to know our future....not compassionate enough to care what we're going through.

Tim Keller shared this idea in a sermon. "Imagine the distance between the earth and our sun (one of the smallest stars) was represented by the width of a piece of paper. With that in mind, the distance between us and the next nearest star in our universe would be represented by a stack of papers seventy feet high. And if we measured our universe end to end by the same measurement, we would need a stack of papers three hundred and ten miles in thickness. The Bible says, `Jesus holds all things together by the Word of His power.' And you want to ask this God into your life as your personal *assistant*?"

Yet Jesus told us, as immense as God truly is, that "even the very hairs of your head are numbered." How much time do you spend looking at yourself in the mirror fixing your hair? Some of us don't have to spend much. But others do...a lot.

I don't know how they study this, but it has been estimated that the average woman spends between six and ten days per year JUST dealing with her hair—roughly a week—styling, coloring, curling, cutting, brushing or combing it.

Yet as much time as you or your stylist spend looking at your hair, tell me how many hairs you have right now? I know, I know. Some of us have NONE. But for those who still have hair taking up residence on your head, how many hairs are there?

Ask the person who loves you most in the world how many hairs you have. As much time as they may spend looking at your head, or running their fingers through your hair, even they don't know how many hairs you have!

Of course we can't number them. But God can. And for some

reason, God does! Imagine how close you would have to be to look and count the hairs on their heads. But God stands just that close to you. He knows you really, really well and loves you anyway! That thought alone should ease the pain of anxiety within you. You are greatly cared for, and greatly loved by the God who keeps your world from spinning apart into a billion pieces, and yet knows when your hair sticks in your hairbrush!

God cares about us and thinks about us-a lot! Your are often on His mind. The key to recovering from and overcoming anxiety is making sure He is often on yours! Tim Keller offered this prayer that seems to be fitting as we close:

Lord,
I worry because I forget your wisdom.
I resent because I forget your mercy.
I covet because I forget your beauty.
I sin because I forget your holiness.
I fear because I forget your sovereignty.
You always remember me. Help me to remember you.
Amen...

CHAPTER 20:
BEYOND THE SCARS TO GLORY

Missionary Amy Carmichael spent much of the last two decades of her life bedridden after a fall in India. But while her missionary travels were curtailed, her ministry continued through her writing. During her life, she published a number of wonderful poems, but none more beloved than the one I have included below:

Hast Thou No Scar?
by Amy Carmichael

Hast thou no scar?
No hidden scar on foot, or side, or hand?
I hear thee sung as mighty in the land,
I hear them hail thy bright ascendant star,
Hast thou no scar?
Hast thou no wound?
Yet, I was wounded by the archers, spent.
Leaned me against the tree to die, and rent
By ravening beasts that compassed me, I swooned:
Hast thou no wound?
No wound? No scar?
Yet as the Master shall the servant be
And pierced are the feet that follow Me;

But thine are whole. Can he have follow far
Who has no wound? No scar?

Scars tells stories. Every scar has one. I have a scar on my arm that I very clearly remember receiving. I got pushed into the jagged metal of a junior high school locker by a larger, jealous eight-grader. Apparently I had made eye contact with his girlfriend, and he needed to teach me a lesson! (For the record, I was not guilty).

But I still bear the scar. And recall the story. Other scars tell stories of surgeries and injuries sustained through the years. But like tattoos (and again, for the record, I don't have one), they tell a story and make us unique.

One of the scars of which I am proudest was received recently during an ocean baptism. I was taken by surprise by a wave and a simultaneous undertow. I immersed myself in front of a couple of hundred spectators, and caught myself on one knee. The knee scraped along the rough ocean sand and shells and I came up bleeding.

It was in a precarious area to isolate with a bandage, and the wound kept opening for the next couple of weeks. It resulted in a perfectly round and permanent scar. But it's not a scar I'm ashamed of...not by any means.It is a war wound! I was wounded bearing witness to Jesus in the ordinance of baptism, and whenever someone asks me, that's what I gladly tell them.

Some scars we can wear proudly. I am not as proud of the scar on my arm where I got pushed around by a bully. But my knee is a different story!

Jesus was wounded for our sins. Crushed for our iniquities. Even after the total transformation of His earthly body into an eternal one...a transformation that happened in the tomb...some of the scars in His body remained. I have to believe it was so planned that we will one day, with awe and wonder, be allowed to touch the nail prints in His hands and feet and the scar left by the spearhead in His side.

Songwriter Michael Card wrote of this reality in a song entitled "Known by the Scars:"

The marks of death that God chose never to erase
The wounds of love's eternal war
When the kingdom comes with its perfected sons
He will be known by the scars

Life wounds us and leaves many scars. Some us of are scarred emotionally by a flawed or failed relationship; by the inflicting of abuse; or even by self-inflicted damage. Some of our scars are apparent...and we would even call them grotesque. Others are hidden to the world, but known to us...and to God.

There's a beauty in our scars born from following Jesus. Our lives will not escape wounding and the resultant scars if we follow Jesus closely.

The bodies of the early saints told their testimony in scars. When they endured beatings by mobs, stoning by angry people, interrogation by persecutors...they bore their suffering and received, instead of a medal...a scar. And one day those scars, those stories, the faith that was demonstrated as the wounding was received...will become the stuff of glory!

C. S. Lewis reflected on this issue of the composition of "glory" in his important book, "The Weight of Glory." His essay and thoughts on this topic have come back to me over and over again as I watched my wife's life dwindle with cancer. Physically she seemed so very weak and in the end physically so frail.

Yet, here's what we both knew. "Though our outer person perishes, yet our inner person is being renewed day by day." (2 Corinthians 4:13) She knew the truth of God's Word that said it is "in our weakness that God's strength is made perfect." I reminded her of that as often as I was able...and reminded myself when she was no longer conscious to hear it.

It was the only way I survived with my sanity and heart intact. I could not imagine seeing such a thing and not knowing...not believing with all of my heart...that this wounding; this scarring was earning for her an "eternal weight of glory that far outweighed" all of the trials, and heartache, and ripping apart that her suffering produced.

If that's where you are as you read these words, take heart! If one you love is slipping away from you day after day...if the suffering from the loss of your own health seems brutal and unending and unrelenting...remember this. It may not be beautiful yet, but it is going to be! The scars that we experience turn to testimonies that we own for an eternity to come.

In his classic work, Lewis gives this picture to us to ponder.

It is a serious thing to live in a society of possible gods and goddesses, to remember that the dullest most uninteresting person you can talk to may one day be a creature which, if you saw it now, you would be strongly tempted to worship, or else a horror and a corruption such as you now meet, if at all, only in a nightmare. All day long we are, in some degree helping each other to one or the other of these destinations...You have never spoken to a mere mortal.
(CS Lewis, The Weight of Glory")

Glory, as the Bible describes it in relationship to God, has weight. The Hebrew word for glory, "kabod," is a word that conveys heaviness.Glory has weight. We are familiar with people sometimes who seem to have a "gravitas" about them; a weightiness of importance. "Kabod" is something we reflect from the Father, Who is the "heaviest" and most glorious and most important of all!

But He shares His glory with us. Our life experiences accelerate or diminish that glory. "All have sinned and fall short of the glory of God," the Book of Romans tells us. We have all sinned, and thereby diminish, or "tarnish" the glory of God reflected in us. Some have extinguished the flame to a weak glow, if not eliminated it altogether.

Yet He allows us to remove the tarnish and stain of sin and our inability to reflect His glory through the sacrifice of Jesus for us. And once that opportunity to reflect it is returned to us, we can continue to increase it's "weight" in our lives. This is where our obedience, our scars, our sacrifice, and our suffering builds into us "an eternal weight of glory..." A glory that is not extinguished. A glory that we reflect throughout eternity as the Father shines His Glory in us as He did through Jesus while He was on the earth.

So don't despise your scars. Your wounds. These are the portals through which the glory of God enters and shines in us! And the glory we will know for eternity will be far better, "not worthy to be compared" to the struggles that brought these scars and wounds about.

If we follow a Master with nail-pierced feet, we can expect no less from this world. And we can expect no lesser glory as a result.

As God looked upon His one and only Son
Who never sinned, nor lied, yet was crucified
And after they had slain Him and laid Him in the grave
And the ones He loved had fled into the dark
Then His love and power raised Him
God won the victory
But they only recognized Him by the scars
("Known by the Scars")

CONCLUSION:

BECOMING JESUS-SHAPED PEOPLE

We cannot fully understand the implications of Romans 8:28, "For we know that in all things God works for the good of those who love Him and who are called according to His purpose" unless we go on to the next verse, "for those God foreknew He also predestined to be made in the likeness of His Son." (Romans 8:29)

God is ultimately about the business of making us into "Jesus-shaped" people. The process of discipleship leads the Christ-follower into Christ-like and Christ-glorifying suffering. We are not saved to be rescued from the fire in this life. We are saved to be molded and made into the image of Christ.

When we accept and understand this, our suffering suddenly comes into focus with laser-sharp clarity. The frailty of our bodies, the pain and disease that many endure, the broken hearts and broken relationships that come, the disappointments that visit and don't seem to go away, all point us to a greater glory...not in Heaven but NOW as we become Jesus-shaped.

It is as God begins and continues the process of chipping away our flesh that Christ-in-us can be clearly seen. It is "Christ in you, the hope of glory," Paul reminds us in Colossians 2:7. We are to "fill up the sufferings of Christ," and in that we are made more like Jesus for God to put on display in the world.

And so, through the difficulties of our lives, God goes to work on us; but not in an effort to harm us or destroy us. No, His plan is to perfect us; to bring us to the point where He can look at us with pleasure as sees His own glorious reflection shining back! Though sin had sold us cheap, the One Who first owned us is shaping His Son in us. And the Letter of Philippians confirms that "He Who began a good work in you will be faithful to complete it..." (Philippians 2:12)

We are, according to 1 Corinthians 15 and other places the "harvest" that comes after the "first fruit" has been given. "Firstfruits" in the Bible were always the best of the crops, the firstborn and unblemished animal, and symbolically the firstborn son. These "firstfruits" were to be offered to God as a sin offering. The firstborn male was to be "redeemed," or bought back by the parents within eight days of his birth.

Jesus was God's "firstfruits." He was His "best" offering ...the firstfruit offering of His only begotten Son for our sin. And when the third day dawned, He was raised from the dead, the "Firstfuit" of those who sleep. He was, in a real sense, the first of a new kind of humanity. He was a living, walking, breathing model that God used to begin to shape a new people. We are, as Christ-followers, people who are being Christ-shaped and made into His image.

But we must remember the One Who in Whose likeness we are being shaped is One Who is called "a man of sorrows, and acquainted with grief." Jesus Himself reminded the disciples that "the servant is not greater than the Master." If the Master was mistreated, persecuted, and brought to suffering then the servant can expect no less to come.

Jesus-shaped people share His cross, His pain, His shame, His struggle. To be made like Jesus, conformed into His likeness, is to be allowed and even caused to suffer as He did. He did not suffer for us to keep us from pain and hardship. "But in this world, you will have tribulation," Jesus said.

Partly our sorrows and suffering come to us because the world that hated Jesus will also hate those who are Jesus-shaped people. "All who live godly lives will suffer persecution." We are not suffering-exempt because of Jesus; we are now predisposed and, to use the Bible's terminology, even predestined to suffering in order to be shaped like Jesus!

In summary, then, our struggles and suffering in life are never intended to destroy us, but to shape us into the image of Christ. "Christ in you, the hope of glory." (Colossians 2:7) We wish for all of life to be one of ease with little in the way of bumps and bruises as we go. In fact that is exactly what many believe today—that God simply exists to make us happy and to ease the journey of our lives along.

And yet, something eternal and God-breathed is happening in the ordinary struggles of every saint of God. Something of our flesh is being chipped away, and something of eternal though for now, invisible grandeur is being etched into us.

We are becoming Jesus-shaped! But such shaping does not occur meaningfully if we are constantly expecting to be delivered from the flames, but only as we are allowed under our Father's watchful eye to linger in them until we are perfected. Then, in the heat of our sufferings, a watching world can begin to see the image of Christ appear in us and His eternal purpose for which we were predestined and created can come to pass. And even *with* our scars, and maybe *because* of our scars, we will be like Jesus.

"Therefore, we do not lose heart."

AFTERWORD

God is Greater

(Given at Jacksonville Association Annual Meeting, Oct 4 2018)

I believe that I shall look[a] upon the goodness
of the Lord in the land of the living!

"God is great, God is good...now we thank Him for our food." This was one of the earliest prayers we taught our kids to say around the dinner table. As they got a little older, we moved the simple prayer into the singing of a chorus, "God is so good...He's so good to me."

I was unaware, though a pastor and a student of theology, that I was introducing in my children one of the most profound theological principles that we will ever ponder: God. Is. Good. All the time. Every time. In any and every circumstance. We believe that, but we don't often think about what we're saying.

We're saying, "God is still good, even when our circumstances aren't. Even when life and providence turn cold and bitter, God continues to show us He is good.

And then, when we add the five letter word "great" to our affirmation, that "God is great and God is good," we add a dimension of complexity. As we taught our children by sheer repetition to affirm before the first bite of mac and cheese or the first morsel of fish sticks to enter their mouths, (though comedian Jon Crist probably has a rule about that), we asked them to recite a mouthful of theology.

Because if God is indeed GOOD (and we believe He is), and God is also GREAT (which we believe as well), then we are affirming that God stands over every circumstance of our lives with an unchangeable goodness and an unchallenged greatness. "And we believe that in all things God is working (greatness) for good for those who love Him...."

The question that emerges from this enormous affirmation is this: "If God is indeed great, and God is indeed good, how can He allow the pain, the difficulty, the inexplicable and heart-wrenching, and sometimes nightmarish issues to occur that happen to us? Especially in the lives of those who are His children? His chosen ones?"

In the Fall of 2016 and into the early months of 2017 our church adopted almost as a constant theme the song, "Good, Good Father." They loved it. It became a heartsong for our family at Fruit Cove. And it sang my family and our congregation into an experience that would test whether or not we really believed what we were singing so heartily.

The day after Easter, my wife was to undergo a surgical procedure to attempt to debulk and biopsy a brain tumor which they already about ten days earlier had diagnosed as a Stage 4 Glioblastoma...ironically the same cancer that had taken my father's life fifteen years before.

We knew when we heard the word "glioblastoma" that Pam had just essentially received a death sentence. The surgery was offered to attempt to remove as much of it as possible and prolong her life for a bit. Of course we were eager to undertake it.

When we got the diagnosis at Mayo Clinic a week or so before, I immediately had an impression from the Lord that my ministry focus was about to shift from pastoring and leading a congregation to taking care of my wife, my soul-mate and partner in ministry of 40 years. When the surgery was planned, there was no doubt our lives were going to radically change, and quickly.

It was not a difficult decision really. There was no choice. I had taken Pam away from her home and family almost 40 years prior. We had no one near us except our son Dave, and it was all he and his wife with a not-quite one year old could say grace over to work and care for her. Our daughter was in Alabama.

So I knew things had to transition. Now I'm confident that every minister/pastor's wife reading this will mutter at least a quiet "amen" under her breath when I say what I'm about to say next.

As shepherds of God's people, we are continually challenged to balance family/church duties...time, energy and focus. In our almost 40 years of marriage I knew I had said "no" to my wife and children five times to one to saying "no" to my church. And I knew with equal confidence that it was now time to say "no" to the church and people I truly loved, so that I could say "yes" to the one God had given me as a wife, ministry partner, and soulmate.

And so on the highest of holy days in the church, Easter Sunday 2017, I had to stand and speak to my church of crucifixion. I didn't plan the timing. But as I closed a brief message on the resurrection, I shared with our church and the assorted guests who gathered that as of the end of the morning, I would be stepping away from the church I had pastored for almost 25 years. The tears flowed and the grief hung in the air.

I called it a leave of absence but was fully prepared to just re-tire early if that was what caring for my bride required. I hadn't done the math, and didn't know how that would even work, but I had ab-solute assurance that being by her side was what I was now being called to do.

In the past years, I had spoken often to my church about suf-fering. Often I speak in funerals about the fact that we are "earthen vessels" that are finite and that rest in the Potter's Hands. Sometimes our vessels decay, and weaken, and crack. And in His plan, the treasure of Christ securely with us, His Light escapes.

There is a purpose...a plan in our suffering. All of it. I have said that for years. I often remind myself and hurting people of Paul's word in 2 Corinthians 12 as he prayed to have his thorn in the flesh removed that God said, "My grace is sufficient for you...for my strength is made perfect in your weakness."

Now it was our turn to illustrate it, however imperfectly. Pam and I had both experienced cancer before. We had been through the crushing fear of hearing those words spoken over us. Neither of those times turned out to be life-threatening. This time was different. A different level of crushing...of crucifixion was about to be experienced.

And here was the problem that we carried with us throughout this trial. How much of our pain do we share? What do we shield? What do we reveal?

I have always practiced transparency with the church. As many who preach tend to do, I used my family often as illustrations in my sermons. It kept things real for me and for the church. When my kids were smaller, they loved hearing their names and stories about themselves from the pulpit. When they got a little older, they became more self-conscious.

So I bribed them. I didn't want to give up good material, so I started paying for it. Literally. My deal was if I used any of them in an illustration but did not first gain their permission to use the story, I would give them $5. It kept me honest, and I would have paid a lot of royalties especially if I used it in two services! Even my wife would charge me!!

Let me tell you something. It made them listen carefully to my sermons! Especially if they thought there was a payoff coming. When my kids got older and moved away they would still charge me if they heard it online. My son and daughter -in love are planning to send their daughter to college on the proceeds from all the McCail stories I use. I tell the church I hope they appreciate what this story is costing me!

And listen. Transparency is costly. Authenticity isn't cheap.

That's why it doesn't happen a lot in the pulpit. Just as the church is a great plac to hide from people who we really are, the pulpit is better. And one more thing...that's why so many in ministry are broken. We won't share the darkness inside of us...the doubts or questions. I would suggest we may have an unhealthy image of what a pastor is.

I am not by nature a person who likes to show strong emotion, either in private and certainly not in public. So don't hear what I'm saying today as from a person for whom this comes easy. It isn't! Sometimes I'd rather donate a kidney than unmask in front of people...and let them see my weakness and my struggles.

But the past few years have changed that about me. Pam used to beg me to ask the church to pray for me when I would undergo some test or medical procedure. "No way." Wouldn't do it.

And when I was diagnosed with prostate cancer, and was facing surgery and a month of recuperation, I still struggled with telling what was happening. It was prostate cancer folks. PROSTATE CANCER! No dignified man wants to stand up in front of a mixed group and talk about his prostate.

But there I was. And the breaking of my pride, and the dying of my flesh had begun. In the same way Christ's flesh died in public, so must ours.

As our journey through dealing with cancer continued through weeks of rehab at Brooks and the discouragement of received pathology that told us essentially there was no treatment available that would address the cancer and she had 3-6 months to live, we had to make a decision: How much of this...how much of our pain...do we disclose and how much do we keep to ourselves?

By this time Pam was permanently in a wheelchair, and unable to use or feel her right side. It was the most painful experience I had ever undergone to watch her seek to regain some movement through long and discouraging rehab visits and exercise at home.

How could I talk about this? What do I share? Added to this the location of Pam's tumor affected her ability to process emotionally so we needed even more to isolate her from the church family she loved.

What I learned and didn't really think about was that the church was grieving too. Our staff and deacons and friends but really everybody who knew us was waiting for any word since I had disappeared following Easter Sunday.

But in my pain, I had withdrawn. In the chaos inside of her, Pam didn't want anybody to know what she was really going through. IN the time when I needed to be most transparent, it was too painful to share.

I'm not sure of everything I was thinking. In the three months after Pam's funeral service, I got in my car and drove off the radar. I ping-ponged back and forth across the southeast, visited a cabin in Blue Ridge, Georgia, my family in Kentucky and West Virginia, even a friend who lived in a cabin on the highest mountain in Georgia!

As I drove, I processed through the questions, my pain, and maybe the most pressing question of all: Do I go back? Honestly, I didn't want to. The church was gracious and offered a sabbatical until the end of 2017. But still I got texts and emails and Facebook posts pressing the question: " Pastor, what are you going to do?"

Frankly, I was done. I was so broken and so weary and so deep in grief coming back was the last thing I could imagine. I wanted to quit.

In that time, I sought counsel from several people I had known and trusted through the years. I was looking for any of them to tell me, "You're right. You're done. Give it up. You're too wounded, too broken to come back."

One of those precious brothers was my best friend who I had walked with over many miles and even through literal and spiritual deserts hit me the hardest. My friend whose pseudonym is Nik Ripken, knew me best. I had walked with him and his wife through the death of their son while on the mission field. He was 16 and we had prearranged the marriage of my daughter and him. He called us before sunrise on

Easter Sunday morning in 1997... the day we opened our brand new worship center.

They wept on the phone with us from Nairobi, Kenya and we walked with them over the next months and years through all the painful circumstances of their crucifixion in burying a beloved son on the mission field

His voice was the one now reassuring me. He said, "Tim, God is great. And He is able to turn this crucifixion into a resurrection if you'll let him. The greatest testimony you will ever have is to be willing to let your congregation who loves you and who loved Pam so well through this, see your scars...your wounds...your pain. You don't have the right to hide this from them. They need to see you're human...and you're hurting. And maybe when you do that, they can find healing for their own wounds. You and I are wounded healers. We all are. And so was Jesus. Don't wait until you're well again to go back to them. How else will they know that God is big enough to handle even this? Tim, don't waste this."

And so, I returned. I agreed to come back later in the fall of 2017...six months after Pam's surgery....two months after her passing. I was raw. I wept openly...I didn't pretend to be strong or not broken. I let the church see the wounds. How great is our God? He took the most broken person He could find whose heart had been shattered into pieces...and in the weakness of this broken pottery began to mend and heal the hearts of a broken church as their tears, and prayers, and concern began to heal mine.

I lost a lot, temporarily. I know where Pam is. But God began the process of building me back piece by piece. How great is our God? He proved that once again, He can turn crucifixion into resurrection...the worst that sin and sorrow and Satan can bring...and use it for His glory.

During my wandering I started pulling together notes and blogs and completed my first book. The proceeds benefit the Cove Center that we hope to open in 2019. Pam made me make a promise...one to write a book that I've been threatening to do for years. Second, to make sure that McCail wouldn't forget her. I did both together.I wrote a book about our experience called I *Bear Witness,* dedicated to our granddarlin, McCail Violet.

Last week at my house, she plopped down on the sofa next to a table with the book on it. For the first time, she picked up the book she's too young to read, but one by one she started through the pages, pointing out family she recognized...and she pointed to Mamaw over and over and over again.

God. Is. Greater.

He is greater than cancer, greater than your failures, greater than your depression, greater than money problems, greater than any loss or any illness or any disease or any sin.

And in the suffering, the death, and the resurrection of Jesus, He proved in. In our suffering, our crucifixion and our resurrection from the ashes, He proves time and again,

God. Is. Good.

BIBLIOGRAPHY

Adamson, Heath. *Grace in the Valley*. Grand Rapids: Baker Books, 2018.

Alcorn, Randy. *Heaven*. Wheaton, IL: Tyndale House, 2004.

If God is Good. Portland: Multnomah Press, 2015.

Carson, D.A. *Praying with Paul*. Grand Rapids: Baker Books, 2014.

Chan, Francis. *Letters to the Churches*. Colorado Springs: David C. Cook, 2018.

Colson, Charles. *The Faith*. Grand Rapids: Zondervan, 2008.

Hughes, Phillip Edgcomb. *The Book of Revelation*. Grand Rapids: Wm B. Eerdmans, 1990.

Keller, Phillip. *A Shepherd Looks at the 23rd Psalm*. Grand Rapids: Zondervan, 2019.

Lewis, C. S. *A Grief Observed*. New York: Harper Collins, 1961.

The Weight of Glory. New York: Harper and Collins, 1976.

Lucado, Max. *Anxious for Nothing*. Nashville: Thomas Nelson, 2017.

Miller, Calvin. *Into the Depths of God*. Minneapolis: Bethany House, 2000.

Metzger, Bruce. *Breaking the Code*. Nashville: Abington Press, 1990.

Morgan, Robert. *Worry Less, Live More*. Nashville: W. Publishing, 2017.

Ortberg, John. *Eternity is Now in Session*. Carol Stream: Tyndale House, 2018.

It All Goes Back in the Box. Grand Rapids: Zondervan, 2008.

Smith, Scotty and Michael Card. *Unveiled Hope*. Nashville: Thomas Nelson, 1997.

Stroebel, Lee. *The Case for Hope*. Grand Rapids: Zondervan, 2015.

Tripp, Paul David. *Suffering: Gospel Hope When Life Doesn't Make Sense*. Wheaton, 2018.

Tozer, A. W. *The Pursuit of God*. Chicago: Moody Press, 1946.

ABOUT THE AUTHOR

Dr. Tim Maynard has served as lead pastor of the Fruit Cove Baptist Church in St. Johns, Florida since 1993. A pastor in Kentucky and Florida for forty years, Tim also serves as adjunct professor for the Baptist College of Florida in Graceville and has served as adjunct professor of Pastoral Care and Counseling for the New Orleans Baptist Theological Seminary. In his spare time, Tim loves biking, playing drums, and hanging out with his granddarlin, McCail Violet. His daughter Allison is married to Patrick Martin who also serves as a pastor in Florida. His son Dave resides in St Johns, Florida where he teaches art in St Johns County at Freedom Crossing. Dave's wife Logan is in management with the Bank of America.

CPSIA information can be obtained
at www.ICGtesting.com
Printed in the USA
FFHW010045060319